Lecture Notes in Computer Science 11381

Commenced Publication in 1973
Founding and Former Series Editors:
Gerhard Goos, Juris Hartmanis, and Jan van Leeuwen

More information about this series at http://www.springer.com/series/7408

Sunita Chandrasekaran
Guido Juckeland · Sandra Wienke (Eds.)

Accelerator Programming Using Directives

5th International Workshop, WACCPD 2018
Dallas, TX, USA, November 11–17, 2018
Proceedings

 Springer

Editors
Sunita Chandrasekaran (iD)
Department of Computer and Information
Science
University of Delaware
Newark, DE, USA

Sandra Wienke (iD)
RWTH Aachen University
Aachen, Nordrhein-Westfalen, Germany

Guido Juckeland (iD)
Helmholtz-Zentrum Dresden-Rossendorf
Dresden, Sachsen, Germany

ISSN 0302-9743   ISSN 1611-3349 (electronic)
Lecture Notes in Computer Science
ISBN 978-3-030-12273-7   ISBN 978-3-030-12274-4 (eBook)
https://doi.org/10.1007/978-3-030-12274-4

Library of Congress Control Number: 2018968279

LNCS Sublibrary: SL2 – Programming and Software Engineering

This Springer imprint is published by the registered company Springer Nature Switzerland AG
The registered company address is: Gewerbestrasse 11, 6330 Cham, Switzerland

2018: 5th Workshop on Accelerator Programming Using Directives (WACCPD)
http://waccpd.org/

Current hardware trends lead to ever more complex compute node architectures offering multiple, heterogeneous levels of massive parallelism. As a result the 'X' in MPI +X demands more focus. A node in a future exascale system is expected to consist of GPU-like accelerators combined with processor architectures of other types. In order to exploit the maximum available parallelism out of such systems, we are in dire need of sophisticated programming approaches that can provide scalable as well as portable solutions without compromising on performance. The expectation from the scientific community is that such solutions should allow programmers to maintain a single code base whenever possible and to avoid requiring maintaining and debugging multiple versions of the same code.

Raising the abstraction of the code is one of the effective methodologies to reduce the burden on the programmer. At the same time such a methodology will require a heroic compiler to be designed. Software abstraction-based programming models such as OpenMP and OpenACC have been serving this purpose over the past several years. These programming models address the 'X' component by providing programmers with high-level directive-based approaches to accelerate and port scientific applications to heterogeneous platforms. Such programming paradigms played a decisive role in establishing heterogeneous node architectures as a valid choice for a multitude of HPC workloads.

The focus of this workshop is to explore this 'X' component in a hybrid MPI +X programming approach. We are looking forward to technical papers discussing innovative high-level language features and their (early prototype) implementations needed to address hierarchical heterogeneous systems, stories and lessons learnt while using directives to migrate scientific legacy code to parallel processors, state-of-the-art compilation and runtime scheduling techniques, techniques to optimize performance, as well as mechanisms to keep communication and synchronization efficient.

WACCPD has been one of the major forums for bringing together users, developers, and the software and tools community to share knowledge and experiences to program emerging complex parallel computing systems.

The WACCPD 2018 workshop received 12 submissions out of which six were accepted to be presented at the workshop and published in the proceedings. The Program Committee of the workshop comprised 26 members spanning university, national laboratories, and industries. Each paper received a maximum of four reviews. Four papers were accepted straight away whereas two papers went through a shepherding phase where the authors were asked to revisit and redo the paper based on feedback obtained from reviewers. The authors were given a 7-day window to revise the paper and resubmit for the shepherd to re-review and decide on an acceptance or a rejection for the workshop.

All the 14 authors were also strongly encouraged to add source files for reproducibility purposes, following SC18 guidelines, upon request from reviewers. Three out of six accepted papers were able to add these source files, which the reviewers greatly appreciated.

The program co-chairs invited Jack Wells from ORNL to give a keynote address on "Experiences in Using Directive-Based Programming for Accelerated Computing Architectures." Dr. Jack Wells is the Director of Science for the Oak Ridge Leadership Computing Facility (OLCF), a DOE Office of Science national user facility, and the Titan supercomputer, located at Oak Ridge National Laboratory (ORNL). Wells is responsible for the scientific outcomes of the OLCF's user programs.

Based on rigorous reviews and ranking scores of all papers reviewed, the following paper won the best paper award. The authors of the best paper award also included reproducibility results to their paper, which the WACCPD workshop organizers had indicated as a criterion to be eligible to compete for the best paper award.

- Anmol Padel and Satish Puri (Marquette University, USA)
- "OpenACC-Based GPU Parallelization of Plane Sweep Algorithm for Geometric Intersection"

Emphasizing the importance of using directives for legacy scientific applications, each presenter was given two recently released textbooks on programming models, one on *Using OpenMP – The Next Step* and the other on *OpenACC for Programmers: Concepts & Strategies*.

January 2019   Sunita Chandrasekaran
                                                                               Guido Juckeland
                                                                               Sandra Wienke

Organization

Steering Committee

Barbara Chapman	Stony Brook, USA
Oscar Hernandez	ORNL, USA
Michael Klemm	Intel, Germany
Kuan-Ching Li	Providence University, Taiwan
Satoshi Matsuoka	Titech, Japan
Duncan Poole	OpenACC, USA
Thomas Schulthess	CSCS, Switzerland
Jeffrey Vetter	ORNL, USA

Program Co-chairs

Sunita Chandrasekaran	University of Delaware, USA
Guido Juckeland	HZDR, Germany
Sandra Wienke	RWTH Aachen University, Germany

Program Committee

David Berntholdt	ORNL, USA
James Beyer	NVIDIA, USA
Sridutt Bhalachandra	Argonne National Laboratory, USA
Makus Eisenbach	ORNL, USA
Manisha Gajbe	Intel, USA
Jeff Hammond	Intel Labs, USA
Si Hammond	SNL, USA
Christian Iwainsky	TU Darmstadt, Germany
Adrian Jackson	EPCC, UK
Arpith Jacob	Google, USA
Henri Jin	NASA-Ames, USA
Gabriele Jost	NASA-Ames, USA
Jeff Larkin	NVIDIA, USA
Seyong Lee	ORNL, USA
Kelvin Li	IBM, Canada
C. J. Newburn	NVIDIA, USA
Antonio J. Peña	BSC, Spain
Thomas Schwinge	Mentor Graphics, Germany
Sameer Shende	University of Oregon, USA
Ray Sheppard	Indiana University, USA
Peter Steinbach	Scionics, Germany
Christian Terboven	RWTH Aachen University, Germany

Xiaonan Tian   NVIDIA/PGI, USA
Veronica Vergarra Larrea   ORNL, USA
Cheng Wang   Microsoft, USA
Michael Wolfe   NVIDIA/PGI, USA

Held in conjunction with

SC18: The International Conference for High-Performance Computing, Networking, Storage and Analysis
Dallas, TX
November 11–17, 2018

Contents

Applications

Heterogeneous Programming and Optimization of Gyrokinetic Toroidal Code Using Directives

Wenlu Zhang[1,2], Wayne Joubert[3], Peng Wang[4], Bei Wang[5],
William Tang[5], Matthew Niemerg[6], Lei Shi[1], Sam Taimourzadeh[1],
Jian Bao[1], and Zhihong Lin[1(✉)]

[1] Department of Physics and Astronomy, University of California, Irvine, USA
zhihongl@uci.edu
[2] Institute of Physics, Chinese Academy of Sciences, Beijing, China
[3] Oak Ridge National Lab, Oak Ridge, TN, USA
[4] NVidia, Santa Clara, USA
[5] Princeton University, Princeton, NJ, USA
[6] IBM, New York, USA

Abstract. The latest production version of the fusion particle simulation code, Gyrokinetic Toroidal Code (GTC), has been ported to and optimized for the next generation exascale GPU supercomputing platform. Heterogeneous programming using directives has been utilized to balance the continuously implemented physical capabilities and rapidly evolving software/hardware systems. The original code has been refactored to a set of unified functions/calls to enable the acceleration for all the species of particles. Extensive GPU optimization has been performed on GTC to boost the performance of the particle push and shift operations. In order to identify the hotspots, the code was the first benchmarked on up to 8000 nodes of the Titan supercomputer, which shows about 2–3 times overall speedup comparing NVidia M2050 GPUs to Intel Xeon X5670 CPUs. This Phase I optimization was followed by further optimizations in Phase II, where single-node tests show an overall speedup of about 34 times on SummitDev and 7.9 times on Titan. The real physics tests on Summit machine showed impressive scaling properties that reaches roughly 50% efficiency on 928 nodes of Summit. The GPU + CPU speed up from purely CPU is over 20 times, leading to an unprecedented speed.

Keywords: Massively parallel computing · Heterogeneous programming · Directives · GPU · OpenACC · Fusion plasma · Particle in cell

1 Introduction

Fusion energy would ensure a safe, environmentally friendly, resource conserving power supply for future generations. In an operating fusion reactor, part of the energy generated by fusion itself will serve to maintain the plasma temperature as fuel is introduced. However, to achieve the desired levels of fusion power output, the plasma

© Springer Nature Switzerland AG 2019
S. Chandrasekaran et al. (Eds.): WACCPD 2018 Workshop, LNCS 11381, pp. 3–21, 2019.
https://doi.org/10.1007/978-3-030-12274-4_1

in a reactor has to be heated and maintained to its operating temperature of greater than 10 keV (over 100 million degrees Celsius) and additional current drive must be applied. Confinement of such a high density and high temperature burning plasma poses big scientific and technological challenges. One critical mission for the fusion energy research and development is the timely achievement of the capability to understand, predict, control, and mitigate performance-limiting and integrity-threatening instabilities in the burning plasmas. The excitation and evolution of the most important instabilities can be expected to depend on kinetic effects and the nonlinear coupling of multiple physical processes spanning disparate spatial and temporal scales.

In the research of fusion plasma physics, simulations have always been an effective tool due to the complexity of theoretical analysis and the high cost of experiments. After several decades of development in the capability of high performance computing, it becomes feasible to conduct massively parallel simulations to investigate the complex physics using equilibrium and profiles close to realist discharges in fusion devices. Along with the progress in computing power, a set of gyrokinetic theory [1–11] have been proposed and established to construct a set of simple theoretical and numerical model by eliminating the fine-scale gyro-phase dependence through gyro-averaging, which reduces the original phase space dimensionality from six to five. This not only assists in the comprehension of the low frequency physics in magnetized plasmas, such as the anomalous transport that is critical for the magnetic fusion, but also facilitates the development and application of massively parallel simulation codes.

As a well benchmarked massively parallel gyrokinetic toroidal code, GTC [12, 13] is built upon the first-principles and adopts efficient low-noise numerical simulation methods for integrated simulations of key instabilities. This is of great significance since these instabilities not only limit the burning plasma performance but also threaten device integrity in magnetic fusion such as the International Thermonuclear Experimental Reactor (ITER) [14], which is a crucial next step in the quest for the fusion energy. The particle-in-cell method is utilized so that particles are treated with a Lagrangian scheme while fluid moments and field information are calculated with an Eulerian scheme. The capability of GTC has been extensively expanded and verified to deal with a wide range of physical problems such as neoclassical and turbulence transport [15, 16], energetic particle transport by microturbulence [17, 18], Alfven eigenmodes [19–22], radio frequency heating [23], static magnetic island [24] and current-driven instabilities [25, 26]. Over the years, the GTC code has grown to a prominent code being developed by an international collaboration with many users and contributors from the magnetic fusion energy and high performance computing communities.

GTC is the key production code for several multi-institutional U.S. Department of Energy (DOE) Scientific Discovery through Advanced Computing (SciDAC) project and National MCF Energy R&D Program, for example. GTC is currently maintained and developed by an international team of core developers who have the commit privilege and receives contributions through the proxies of core developers from collaborators worldwide [13]. GTC continuously pushes the frontiers of both physics capabilities and high-performance computing. It is the first fusion code to reach the teraflop in 2001 on the Seaborg computer at NERSC [27] and the petaflop in 2008 on the Jaguar computer at ORNL [16] in production simulations. GTC is also the benchmark and early application code that fully utilizes the computing power of a list of TOP500 machines such as Tianhe-1A [28] and Titan with a CPU and GPU heterogeneous architecture and Tianhe-2 [29] with an Intel Xeon Phi accelerator architecture.

In the pursue of extreme performance from the high computing community, many excellent pioneer works have been carried by computer scientists and developers by porting and optimization the GTC and its companion codes to the GPU on variety of machines. The work of Madduri et al. [30, 31] discussed the porting of an earlier version of GTC to GPU and concluded that the GPU was slower than the CPU for their version of GTC, which only included kinetic ions with adiabatic electrons. Then the GTC GPU [28] version, which was the Tianhe-1A benchmark code developed on the production version using NVidia CUDA libraries, showed some speedup and excellent scaling in the whole machine test with the actual physics simulation parameters. The weak scaling to 3072 nodes of Tianhe-1A was obtained with 2X-3X overall speedup comparing NVidia M2050 GPUs to Intel Xeon X5670 CPUs. A "companion" version of the GTC code, the GTC-P code is a modern, highly portable GTC code now operational on the top 7 supercomputers worldwide [32]. Over the years, GTC-P has been ported and optimized on different supercomputers such as IBM Blue Gene/P (BG/P) at Argonne Leadership Computing Facility (ALCF), IBM Blue Gene/Q (BG/Q) of Mira at ALCF, Sequoia at Lawrence Livermore National Laboratory, the Cray XT4, Cray XE6, and later Cray XC30 at Lawrence Berkeley National Laboratory, et al. [32, 33]. The scalability up to 131,072 BG/P and 32,768 XT4 cores were attained with as little as 512 MB memory per core by incorporating a new radial decomposition method, developed first by Ethier et al. that features a dramatic increase in scalability for the grid work and decrease in the memory footprint of each core [33]. Later, Madduri et al. made further optimizations of the code, such as multi-level particle and grid decompositions, particle binning, and memory-centric optimizations. As a result, they delivered 1.22x, 1.35x, 1.77x, and 1.34x performance improvement on BG/P, the Cray XE6, and Intel Cluster, and a Fermi Cluster, respectively [30]. Recently, the radial domain decomposition was optimized by Wang et al., which enables the GTC-P code scale up to the full capability of Sequoia (98,304 nodes), and Mira (49,152 nodes) [32]. The performance was increased from nearly 50 billion particles per second per step (BPST) to more than 100 BPST on 98,304 Sequoia nodes. GTC-P was also weak scaling to 32,768 Fujitsu K nodes, and about 50 BPST was achieved [34].

In this work, the associated R&D has been focused toward the goal of delivering a comprehensive and modern production version of the fusion GTC code capable of greatly accelerating progress toward a realistic predictive capability for ITER experiments. The technical advances are aimed at providing the computational foundations needed for simulating nonlinear interactions of multiple physical processes covering disparate spatiotemporal scales in burning plasmas. This is part of efforts to develop the next generation applications for exascale supercomputing platforms. For vast portability and easy maintenance, the directive approach is chosen to lower the technical requirement for students and researchers of fusion plasma physics.

GTC is one of a small but growing number of production applications run on leadership class systems to employ compiler directives to access modern accelerated node hardware. Use of compiler directive programming models such as OpenACC and OpenMP is of increasing importance to achieve performance portability across multiple target computer architectures. We believe the lessons learned in this paper will be useful to other developers wishing to use directives for programming to accelerated architectures.

This paper is organized as follows. Section 2 briefly introduces the benchmark platforms of Titan, SummitDev, and Summit. Section 3 discusses the technical basis of the GTC code, which is followed by the porting and optimization strategies in Sect. 4. Section 5 reports the status of the porting and optimization. Section 6 shows the performance benchmarks. The conclusions are given in Sect. 7.

2   Simulation Platforms: Titan, SummitDev, and Summit

All the benchmark runs in the following sections were performed on the Titan, SummitDev, and Summit supercomputers, both hybrid massively parallel processing (MPP) systems with CPUs and GPUs.

The Titan system at Oak Ridge National Laboratory (ORNL) is a Cray XK7 system composed of 200 cabinets containing 18,688 compute nodes, each equipped with a 16-core Advanced Micro Devices AMD Interlagos processor with 32 GB of memory and an NVidia Kepler K20X GPU accelerator with 6 GB memory, with Gemini interconnect. Titan's peak speed is in excess of 27 petaflops. The GPU attains a peak double precision rate of 1.311 TF/s with main memory bandwidth of 250 GB/s and is connected to the CPU by a PCI Express Gen 2.0 bus with an 8 GB/s data transfer rate [41].

SummitDev is an early access system at ORNL used by developers to prepare applications for the 200 PF Summit system to be available in 2018. SummitDev is comprised of 54 IBM Power8 S822LC compute nodes connected with a Mellanox EDR Infiniband network, each node containing two IBM POWER8 processors with 10 cores and 80 hardware threads each. Each CPU is connected by an 80 GB/sec NVLINK connection to two NVidia P100 GPUs with peak double precision rate of 5.312 TF/sec and with 16 GB of on-package high bandwidth memory with peak speed of 732 GB/sec [42].

Summit is the next generation leadership supercomputer at ORNL, which is the 200PF system built upon IBM AC922 architecture. It consists of 4,608 nodes linked with Mellanox EDR 100G InfiniBand network, each node host 2 22-core IBM Power 9 CPUs, 6 Nvidia Volta GPUs, 512 GB DDR4 memory and 96 GB HBM2 memory on GPU.

3   Scientific Methods of GTC

As a gyrokinetic particle-in-cell [35, 36] (PIC) code, GTC tracks individual charged marker particles in a Lagrangian frame in a continuous phase-space [10, 11], whereas the moments of particle distribution of different species (thermal ion, thermal electron, fast ion, fast electron, etc.) are simultaneously computed on a stationary Eulerian field mesh. This field mesh is also used to interpolate the local electromagnetic fields at the marker particle positions in phase-space. The trajectories of charged marker particles (guiding centers) in a strong magnetic field are calculated by integrators of the equations of motion in the self-consistent electromagnetic fields computed on the field mesh. The number density and current density carried by each marker particle is then projected to the field mesh through interpolations. The moments of the distributions of species, such as number density, charge density and current density, are then calculated by accumulating the projected quantities of marker particles. The electromagnetic fields are then solved on mesh grids using proper combinations of Poisson equation, Ampere's law, Faraday's law and force-balance equations with finite difference methods [37] and finite element methods [38].

The PIC approach implemented in GTC dramatically reduces the computation complexity from $O(N^2)$ to $O(N + MlogM)$, where N is the number of particles, and M is the number of grid points [34, 39]. The use of spatial grids and the procedure of gyro-averaging reduce the intensity of small-scale fluctuations (particle noise). Particle collisions can be recovered as a "sub-grid" phenomenon via Monte Carlo methods. The system geometry simulated in GTC is a torus with an externally-imposed equilibrium magnetic field [30]. In order to capture and take advantage of the characteristics of this curvature geometry, GTC employs the magnetic flux coordinate system (ψ, θ, ζ) [40], where ψ is the poloidal magnetic flux, θ is the poloidal angle and ζ is the toroidal angle. This is the base coordinate used for mesh construction, on which the equilibrium and profiles are built. It is also used to construct an intermediate field-line-following coordinate (ψ, θ, α) by a simple transformation $\alpha = \zeta - q(\psi)\theta$, where q is the tokamak safety factor (representing magnetic field-line pitch). The introduction of such a field-line coordinate system makes it convenient to decompose a vector into components parallel and perpendicular to the direction of magnetic field and to separate the rapid guiding center motion along the magnetic field lines from the slow motion across the lines, which promotes the simplicity in theory analysis and efficiency in numerical simulation. In particular, the field-line coordinate system drastically reduced computational complexity in the parallel direction. The Poisson equation can be simplified and solved in the (ψ, θ) plane perpendicular to the equilibrium magnetic field in this field-line coordinate system.

Physical quantities and variables in GTC can be divided into various categories. The first one includes the field quantities bounded to the stationary mesh, such as electrostatic potential, vector potential, magnetic fields, and accumulated number density and current density distributions on mesh. Originally, the field solver was built on the Portable, Extensible Toolkit for Scientific Computation (PETSc), which was the best choice in the dual core and multiple code age and has been the major solver for daily electromagnetic simulations. However, it gradually emerges as a serious

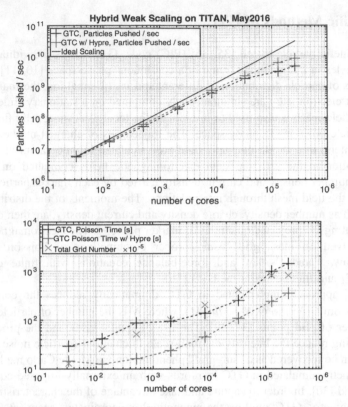

Fig. 1. Phase-I weak scaling of GTC on Titan (top), with the number of nodes ranging from 32 to 16384 (88% of the whole machine). Both grid number and total particle number are increased, but the number of particles per core remains constant. The Poisson time (bottom) shows the improved performance due to the Hypre multigrid solver. The total grid number is also shown.

performance hot spot later in the many-core and heterogeneous architecture era due to its lack of in-node accelerations for many-core architectures, for instance for general purpose GPU and Intel Xeon Phi.

The other category includes marker particle related quantities for every species, such as physical position, velocity or momentum, particle number and electric current carried by each marker particle. Depending on the physics studied, a typical production run in fusion plasma research may have multiple species with different governing equations, such as thermal ions, thermal electrons, energetic ions, energetic electrons, impurities, etc. Originally, each species had its own set of functions and subroutines which are used to calculate the particle trajectories (push subroutine), manage and exchange particle information between computing devices and processes (shift subroutine), and aggregate number density and current density as well as the thermal pressure carried by each particle (charge subroutine).

GTC has successfully transferred the physical models into computing power by employing a multi-level palatalization technique, which utilizes the Message Passing Interface (MPI) to manage and balance the distributed computing resources cross computing nodes or devices on the top level, and utilizes shared memory multiprocessing (SMP) techniques via OpenMP and OpenACC/CUDA inside each node or device on the lower level so that it can take the advantage of the hardware hierarchy of modern massively parallel computers and reach a scale up to millions of conventional CPU cores and heterogeneous accelerating devices such as NVidia GPU and Intel Xeon Phi (MIC) chips.

4 Porting and Optimization Strategy

When porting the GTC code to the next generation supercomputing machines powered by accelerators or co-processors such as the GPU or Intel Xeon Phi (MIC), significant challenges are anticipated. Achieving high parallel efficiency on complex modern architectures is in general a formidable task facing PIC codes because of potential fine-grained data hazards, irregular data access, and low arithmetic intensity. Attaining high performance becomes an increasingly complex challenge as HPC technology evolves towards vast on-node parallelism in modern multi- and many-core designs. In order to harness the computing power of advanced systems such as Summit, application codes, including GTC, need to be carefully designed such that the hierarchy of parallelism provided by the hardware is fully utilized. To this end, the multithreading capabilities in the GTC code will be enhanced.

GTC was originally written in Fortran 90. The current GTC version has four species of particles: thermal ions, fast ions, fast electrons and kinetic thermal electrons. Many routines are shared between those particle types. In fusion simulations using GTC, the number of particles per mesh cell varies from tens to thousands in a typical production run for each particle species, which means that every cell would have O (10)–O(10^3) of particles. In other words, the total number of particles is O(10)–O(10^3) larger than the total number of cells (with field data on cells). Most of the data, either on disk or in memory, and runtime—including I/O time and computing time—are accordingly consumed by the particle routines instead of field routines, which has been consistent with our benchmarking results.

The preceding analysis and observations suggest that particle related routines are the key for optimizing the PIC code like GTC. An appropriate effective strategy for porting GTC to a CPU-GPU heterogeneous architecture would be as follows: migrate all particle relevant data and computing onto the GPU. This approach will not only enable the utilization of the most powerful computing unit of the heterogeneous architecture but also minimize the data transfer between the CPU and the GPU which can be the most challenge part when utilizing GPU in high performance computing. Instead of porting each particle species one by one, all the particle related routines are replaced with a set of unified push, charge and shift routines, which can then be ported to the GPU using OpenACC. After the successful port of particle related part, the field solvers will also be ported onto the GPU to boost the computing performance of field solvers (Figs. 1 and 2).

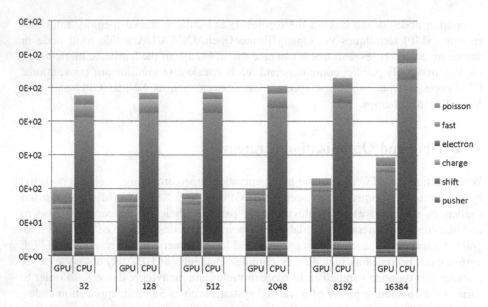

Fig. 2. The Phase I timing breakdown for GTC particle weak scaling study on Titan. Note: x-axis is the number of nodes and y-axis the total wall-clock time. The GPU delivers up to 3.0X speedup compared with the CPU.

Given the existing MPI-OpenMP framework, the most natural parallel framework for GTC on CPU-GPU nodes would be using one MPI rank per GPU. Since the CPU version is already parallelized using OpenMP, OpenMP threads should also be enabled to utilize all the available CPU cores.

A large part of the performance optimization work will thus focus on multi-threading for NVidia GPU and Intel Xeon Phi architectures (MIC), as well as current multicore processors. Fortunately, the GTC code has been using multithreading for more than a decade and has already had initial porting efforts to advanced heterogeneous architecture systems that deploy the GPU and Intel MIC.

To satisfy the needs for performance portability across multiple HPC system architectures, GTC will initially support multiple programming models via conditional compilation. For shared memory multi-core and Intel Xeon Phi many-core processors, OpenMP parallel directives are used. Support for NVidia GPUs will be deployed using OpenACC directives. An alternative conditionally compiled CUDA code path will be available for cases when compilers are not yet able to generate well-performing code for OpenACC. Later as compiler support becomes available, OpenMP 4.5 and 5.0 target directives will be evaluated as a potential performance portability solution.

GTC currently uses the DOE-funded PETSc toolkit to implement the electro-magnetic parallel solvers. PETSc is a well-established MPI-based framework through which many different solvers can be exercised without having to change the source code. Advanced third-party packages, such as LLNL's Hypre multigrid solver, can also be used via the PETSc framework with a simple parameter change in a runtime configuration file. Nevertheless, in spite of its successful use in GTC, PETSc has some limitations with respect to today's advanced computer architectures. The main draw-back is its lack of multithreading support, which especially impacts global PIC codes like GTC since they run routinely in mixed-mode MPI + OpenMP. It would clearly be beneficial to introduce OpenMP multithreading at the lowest level, for example, in the PETSc functions. This would help us avoid having to deal with non-thread-safe issues in higher-level functions.

In order to identify the hotspots and performance issues, code profiling was per-formed to reveal performance characteristics and to identify performance issues. The code's timer instrumentation for major parts of the computation was revised to provide performance data needed for the project (Fig. 3).

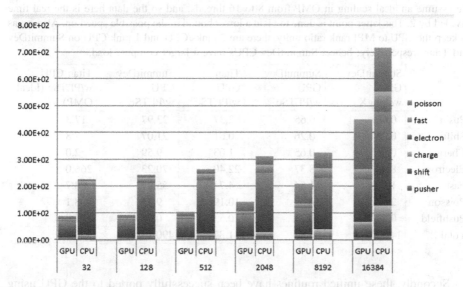

Fig. 3. The Phase I timing breakdown for GTC hybrid weak scaling study on Titan. Here the work per processor is increased as node count is increased. Note: x-axis is the number of nodes and y-axis the total wall-clock time. GPU delivers up to 3.0x speedup compared with CPU.

5 GPU Porting Status

Baseline code versions were extracted from current production version of GTC (For-tran) as a starting point of the code porting and optimization work. Firstly, all the particle routines (push, charge and shift) for thermal ions, fast ions and fast electrons and kinetic thermal electrons have been replaced by the set of unified routines, which can operate on every species controlled by the calling parameters like:

```
push(species_name, and other parameters)
charge(species_name)
shift(species_name)
```

where species_name is the description keyword which can be any of "thermal-ion", "thermal-electron", "fast-ion" or "fast-electron". Such species, including both the thermal and fast particles, are described by diverse physical models such as fully-kinetic, gyrokinetic, drift-kinetic, or fluid-kinetic hybrid. This makes it possible that all species benefit from optimizations, for example OpenACC optimizations for the GPU, through changing only one subroutine.

Table 1. Phase II GPU and CPU timings (in seconds) from the preliminary SummitDev benchmarks. For comparison, the same physics case, for both GPU and CPU, is shown for Titan. All runs use 32 MPI ranks; GPU runs have 1 GPU/MPI rank; the SummitDev CPU run has 5 OMP/MPI rank; and the Titan CPU case has 8 OMP/MPI rank, however in the data shown here, we assume an ideal scaling in OMP from 8 to 16 threads, and so the data here is the real time divided by 2. This latter point is done to yield a lower bound in the possible speed up. Also, so as to keep the GPU to MPI rank ratio unity, there are 2 ranks/CPU and 1 rank/CPU on SummitDev and Titan, respectively; hence, SummitDev CPUs have a larger compute load.

	SummitDev GPU w/AmgX	SummitDev GPU w/PETSc	Titan GPU w/PETSc	SummitDev CPU w/PETSc	Titan CPU w/PETSc (Ideal OMP)
Pushi	0.66	0.65	2.37	23.97	17.3
Shifti	0.26	0.26	0.61	21.07	7.8
Chargei	0.66	0.65	1.03	9.59	2.0
Electron	8.40	8.37	22.40	370.23	266.0
Fast	1.53	1.54	4.74	55.47	28.7
Poisson	2.64	14.67	10.19	9.54	8.1
Pushfield	0.27	0.27	0.53	0.26	1.0
Total	14.42	26.41	41.87	490.13	330.9

Secondly, these unified routines have been successfully ported to the GPU using OpenACC directives supported by PGI compiler. GTC's main data structure is allocatable arrays within modules. The "acc declare" directive was used in the module file to specify all the arrays that the GPU needs to access. Then, the CPU code for allocating the array typically will not require any change since the OpenACC runtime will automatically allocate a GPU copy if an array is specified in "acc declare". Whenever data needs to be copied between the CPU and the GPU, the "acc update" directive was used. Finally, the "acc host_data" directive was used to interoperate with the CUDA kernels.

The unified push routine was ported to the GPU using OpenACC. Most of the push time is spent in two loops. The first loop performs a gather operation from grid points to particles. By porting this loop to CUDA, it was identified that using texture cache for the grid arrays will lead to ~3X speedup compared to the base OpenACC version. So, enabling texture cache in OpenACC will be an important next step for optimizing this loop. The second loop updates the particle locations. It was identified that the memory access of the private array "dx" was the main bottleneck. This "dx" array stores the coefficients used to interpolate the local field quantities from the Euclidian meshes.

The optimization was to move the array bound variable for dx to a module file as a parameter and rewrite some of the loops involving dx using the array bound parameter. Those changes enabled the compiler to put this array in local memory, which led to ~ 4X speedup compared to the base OpenACC version. So, this made a case for adding texture cache support to OpenACC. Experimental support of texture cache is now being added to PGI's OpenACC compiler, and we will test it when available.

The unified charge routine was ported to the GPU using OpenACC. Because different particles may write to the same grid points, the OpenACC atomic directive was used to handle write collisions. This strategy looked to be working well.

The shift routine was ported to CUDA before the US DOE Center for Accelerated Application Readiness (CAAR) program. Since shift routine is not modified by developer often at all, the GTC team thinks it's fine to use the CUDA version for this routine. So, the CUDA port in previous version was used for shift routine.

A binning subroutine, based on the out-of-place counting sort algorithm, was implemented in GTC (radial_bin.F90). The first version of the binning algorithm bins all particle species in the radial dimension periodically to improve data locality for charge deposition and field interpolation. For linear problems, where spatial change is small in the radial dimension from one time step to the next, up to 10% overall speedup is observed. It is expected that binning will speed up the performance significantly for nonlinear problems. Later, a cell-based binning was developed and improved the performance by 70% for electron subroutines. Overall, over 10% performance improvement is observed by enabling the cell-based binning.

Both Array of Structure (AoS) and Structure of Array (SoA) data layouts for particles have been implemented on a simplified version of GTC. For GPU, performance analysis is conducted using CUDA profiling toolkit nvprof on a single Titan node. Higher bandwidth and transactions are observed for the AoS layout. Overall no significant speedup is obtained with the SoA data structure for all versions including CPU, GPU (OpenACC) and GPU (CUDA) of the code. We thus decide to use AoS layout for all particle species (as before). The SoA alternative will be available in the future for architectures for which this data layout might improve performance.

Due to increasing relative costs of the Poisson field solve, the PETSc standard solver has been replaced with several alternatives. The Hypre algebraic multigrid solver, whether used standalone or as part of PETSc, runs up to 11X faster than the PETSc standard solver on SummitDev. An early GPU-enabled version of Hypre gave up to 15X improvement over PETSc, and furthermore the NVidia AmgX solver executed up to 27X faster than PETSc. The new solvers also scale much better than PETSc, an increasingly important property as larger and more complex problems are attempted.

GTC uses explicit OpenACC directives to manage GPU data. Unified memory has been introduced since CUDA 6.0 for reducing the complexity of GPU programming and improving performance through data locality. Though typical unified memory implementation has lower performance than explicit memory management, it is interesting to port GTC to unified memory to evaluate the tradeoff between productivity and performance. The initial experiments have suggested that using unified memory in GTC incurred a significant performance penalty due to page fault of Fortran automatic arrays. It is expected that the performance of the unified memory will be improved as PGI provides optimized pool allocator.

Table 2. Phase II GPU speedups, for 15 time steps. SummitDev speedups are relative to the SummitDev CPU w/PETSc & 5 OMP thread/rank case. The Titan GPU speedup is relative to the Titan CPU w/PETSc & Ideal OMP case (see Table 1 caption). All GPU runs use 32 MPI, with 1 GPU/rank.

	SummitDev GPU w/AmgX, Speed up	SummitDev GPU w/PETSc, Speed up	Titan GPU w/PETSc, Speed up
Pushi	36.2	36.6	7.3
Shifti	82.5	80.5	12.7
Chargei	14.6	14.7	1.9
Pushe	27.4	27.6	14.0
Shifte	76.1	75.9	9.6
Chargee	10.2	10.2	2.7
Fast	36.2	36.0	6.0
Poisson	3.6	0.7	0.8
Pushfield	1.0	1.0	1.8
Total	34.0	18.6	7.9

6   Performance

A set of test problems was developed for evaluating performance (see scaling studies below). The physics case [21] in the 2013 Physical Review Letters by Wang et al. was prepared as a base case to measure improvements in performance. This choice is appropriate since it is a good representation of future production runs and GTC's capabilities, since it employs all particle species, electromagnetic capabilities, experimental profiles and realistic tokamak equilibrium.

6.1   Solver Performance Improvement

The GTC Poisson solver currently runs on the CPU. Though it is presently not the most time-consuming part of GTC simulations, the solver time requirements have become more significant since other parts of the code have been accelerated using GPUs. We have replaced the standard PETSc solver with a Hypre multigrid solver. This solver is threaded to effectively use the CPUs and is also scalable to many compute nodes. Figure 1 shows comparative timings of the PETSc solver and the Hypre multigrid solver for a representative set of GTC test cases. The Hypre solver for these cases is ∼4X faster than the standard PETSc solver and has better scaling properties.

6.2   Scaling Performance

Two sets of weak scaling studies were carried out on Titan up to nearly the full system (16,384 nodes; at the time of this study, many Titan nodes were unavailable, making it impossible to run on all 18,688 nodes). The first test set is called "particle weak scaling study", where we fix the grid size, but scale the total number of particles. The second set of tests is called "hybrid weak scaling study", where we scale both the grid size and total number of particles. The first study holds the number of particles per MPI rank and the number of grid cells per MPI rank nearly constant, thus reflecting a conventional weak scaling study; the second study is a more realistic scaling study based on typical production run of the code: grid size is proportional to the square root of number of nodes. For both sets of weak scaling study, the number of particles per processor is fixed at 3.2 million. Compared with CPU (16 cores AMD 6274), GPU (NVidia K20x) has boosted the overall performance by 1.6–3.0X. The decrease of the performance speedup in large processor counts is mainly due to the increased portion of the non-GPU accelerated subroutines as well as MPI time. These tests were conducted in May 2016 (Fig. 4).

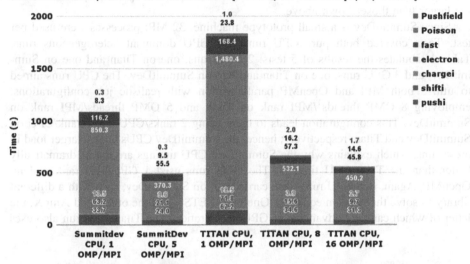

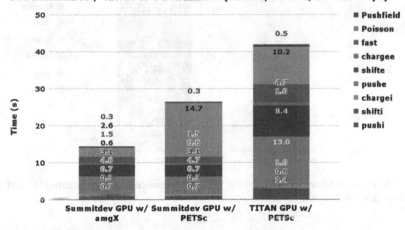

Fig. 4. The Phase II timing breakdown for GTC performance study on SummitDev and Titan for 15 time steps and 32 MPI processes. Note that in order to keep the GPU to MPI ratio unity, there are 2 ranks/CPU and 1 rank/CPU on SummitDev and Titan, respectively. Hence, SummitDev CPUs have a larger load. (Top) Pure CPU tests with a scan of OMP thread/rank. (Bottom) GPU tests. All GPU runs use 1 GPU/rank.

6.3 Tests on SummitDev

To foreshadow the performance of GTC on the next generation supercomputer, Summit, a set of dedicated benchmarks have been executed on SummitDev and Titan, again employing the physics case used in Sect. 6.1. The scaling study of Sect. 6.2 was executed in May 2016, and since then much effort has been placed into GTC's GPU optimizations, such as removing unnecessary CPU to GPU data transfer and an increase in compiler support for texture, for use on Titan, and these additions have subsequently been ported for use on SummitDev. Hence, the speedups presented here are larger than those shown above.

Since SummitDev is a small prototype machine, 32 MPI processes were used per test. Tests covered both pure CPU runs and GPU dominant heterogeneous runs. Table 1 tabulates the results of 5 tests: 2 CPU runs, one on Titan and one on SummitDev, and 3 GPU runs, one on Titan and two on SummitDev. The CPU runs aimed to utilize both MPI and OpenMP parallelization with realistic job configurations, employing 8 OMP threads[1]/MPI rank on Titan and 5 OMP threads/MPI rank on SummitDev. This configuration leads to there being 2 ranks/CPU and 1 rank/CPU on SummitDev and Titan, respectively; hence, the SummitDev CPUs have a larger load in these runs, which explains why the SummitDev CPU timings are not as dramatically better than the Titan CPU timings. The GPU runs used 1 GPU/MPI rank and no OpenMP. Again, two GPU runs were carried out on SummitDev, each with a different library to solve the Poisson equation. One used PETSc, and the other used AmgX, the latter of which can take advantage of GPU acceleration. The Titan GPU run also uses

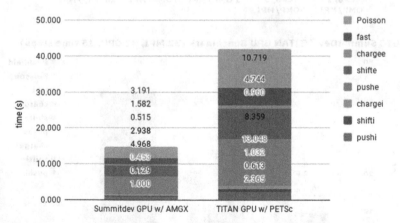

Fig. 5. The Phase II timing breakdown for GTC performance study on SummitDev and Titan for 15 time steps and 32 MPI processes.

---

[1] The timings for the TITAN CPU w/PETSc case in Table 1 assume an ideal scaling in OMP threads from 8 threads to 16. i.e. the times presented in Table 1 for this case are those of the 8 OMP threads case, but they are divided by 2. The motivation for this is to set a lower bound in the possible GPU speedup attainable in TITAN.

PETSc to solve the Poisson equation. With AmgX, the total number of particles pushed per second on the SummitDev GPU run is 1.29×10^9.

The tabulated data is also presented in Fig. 4. The upper panel shows CPU only tests on both SummitDev and Titan for a range of OMP threads/MPI rank. The scaling from 8 to 16 OMP threads/MPI rank in Titan was poor. This is in part due to there being a decrease in efficiency when using OMP threads across cores on Titan–hence we assumed an ideal scaling from 8 to 16 OMP threads/MPI rank in Table 1 to obtain a lower bound in the possible speedup attainable. The lower panel presents the GPU timing data (Fig. 5).

Table 2 shows the GPU speedups obtained. SummitDev GPU speedups are relative to the SummitDev CPU case with 5 OMP threads/MPI rank, and Titan GPU speedups are relative to the Titan CPU case with ideal OMP scaling from 8 to 16 threads/MPI rank. The overall speedups were 34.0 and 18.6 on SummitDev, for the AmgX and PETSc libraries, respectively, and 7.9 on Titan. The most notable speedups came from the particle push and shift routines on SummitDev, with a roughly 36 and 82 times speed up for the ion push and shift, respectively; and a roughly 27 and 76 times speed up for the electron push and shift, respectively. The high speedup factors are to large degree enabled by the very effective use of texture cache as described earlier, as well as need to further optimize the OpenMP threading version for CPU. Moreover, the utilization of the AmgX library decreases the Poisson time by 5.5 times. It is noteworthy that the SummitDev/GPU/AmgX to Titan/PETSc performance ratio is about 3X, roughly in line with the 4X flop rate ratio and 3X memory bandwidth ratio of SummitDev vs. Titan GPUs.

6.4 Performance and Scalability on Summit

For testing the performance and scalability on Summit and the early science applications thereafter, a set of test problems was developed for evaluating performance. The physics simulation reported in [21] was prepared as a base case to measure improvements in performance. As shown in Table 3 and Fig. 6. GTC CPU-only runs scale almost perfectly up to 928 nodes (about 20% of the whole Summit) in the weak scaling test (i.e., by keeping constant number of particles per node). The simulation on 928 nodes uses 2×10^6, i.e., 1 million grids and 2×10^{11} particles utilizing 2/3 of the GPU memory. GTC simulations using all GPUs and CPUs also show good scaling, with a $\sim 50\%$ efficiency at 928 Summit nodes when compared with the ideal scaling. The GTC speed up from CPU-only to GPU + CPU is over 20 at 928 Summit nodes, leading to an unprecedented speed of one trillion particle pushes in 2 s wall-clock time. Furthermore, GTC performance on each Summit GPU is about 8 times faster than each Titan GPU. Finally, as part of the Summit acceptance benchmark simulations, preliminary results of GTC running on 4576 Summit nodes (by Dr. Wayne Joubert of OLCF) show good scaling and similar performance, as shown in Fig. 7. The impressive GTC performance on Summit would enable integrated simulation of multiple physical processes.

Table 3. Wall-clock time for one trillion particle pushes in the GTC weak scaling test on Summit.

Summit nodes	16	64	256	512	928
GPU + CPU	58.43	15.37	4.99	2.92	2.00
CPU only	2167.56	525.98	150.45	71.53	41.76

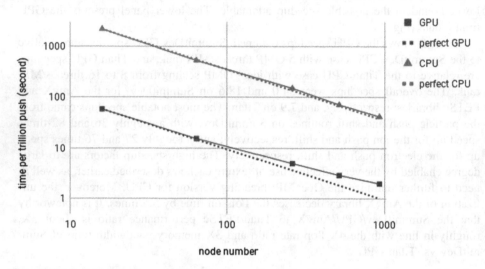

Fig. 6. Wall-clock time for one trillion particle pushes in the GTC weak scaling test on Summit.

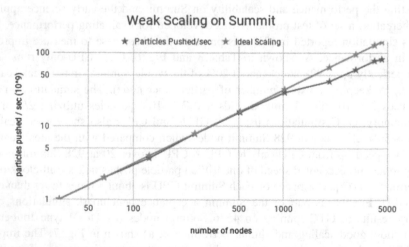

Fig. 7. Phase-II weak scaling of GTC on Summit, with the number of nodes ranging from 32 nodes to 4576 nodes (almost the whole machine). Total particle number are increased by increasing the number of particles per node.

7 Conclusion

We have successfully restructured the current production version of gyrokinetic toroidal code (GTC) to a more modularized format with unified routines for all particle species, including thermal ions, thermal electrons, fast ions and fast electrons. This is followed by the optimizations using OpenACC directives to enable the GPU accelerations, which is also relatively friendly for fusion physics researchers and students. Other techniques have also been introduced to boost the performance to a higher level, which includes the binning technique where particle data storage is optimized for access. Hypre and Amgx have been adopted as alternatives to the PETSc field solver, which make the code benefit from the accelerations of many core CPUs (Hypre) and GPUs (AmgX).

Realistic profiles and parameters from fusion experiments have been used in GTC benchmarks to provide insights into technical interests and scientific significance. The strong and weak scaling studies have been performed and the overall speedup is about 2–3 times with a very good scalability on the whole Titan; and on SummitDev it shows an overall speedup of about 34 times. The real physics tests on Summit machine have also been conducted to tackle the self-consistent energetic particle physics in fusion plasmas, especially for ITER. These tests showed impressive scaling properties that reaches roughly 50% efficiency on 928 nodes which is 20% of total nodes of Summit. The GPU + CPU speed up from purely CPU is over 20 times, leading to an unprecedented speed.

Acknowledgments. The authors would like to thank Eduardo D'Azevedo for his many useful suggestions in the optimizations. This work was supported by the US Department of Energy (DOE) CAAR project, DOE SciDAC ISEP center, and National MCF Energy R&D Program under Grant Nos. 2018YFE0304100 and 2017YFE0301300, the National Natural Science Foundation of China under Grant Nos. 11675257, and the External Cooperation Program of Chinese Academy of Sciences under Grant No. 112111KYSB20160039. This research used resources of the Oak Ridge Leadership Computing Facility (OLCF) at the Oak Ridge National Laboratory, which is supported by the Office of Science of the U.S. Department of Energy under Contract No. DE-AC05-00OR22725.

References

1. Lee, W.W.: Phys. Fluids **26**, 556 (1983)
2. Lee, W.: J. Comput. Phys. **72**, 243 (1987). ISSN 0021-9991
3. Littlejohn, R.G.: J. Plasma Phys. **29**, 111 (1983)
4. Brizard, A., Hahm, T.: Rev. Mod. Phys. **79**, 421 (2007)
5. Hahm, T.: Phys. Fluids (1958–1988) **31**, 2670 (1988)
6. Frieman, E., Chen, L.: Phys. Fluids (1958–1988) **25**, 502 (1982)
7. Rogister, A., Li, D.: Phys. Fluids B: Plasma Phys. (1989–1993) **4**, 804 (1992)
8. Lin, Z., Chen, L.: Phys. Plasmas (1994-present) **8**, 1447 (2001)
9. Lin, Y., Wang, X., Lin, Z., Chen, L.: Plasma Phys. Controlled Fusion **47**, 657 (2005)
10. Holod, I., Zhang, W.L., Xiao, Y., Lin, Z.: Phys. Plasmas **16**, 122307 (2009)
11. Liu, P., Zhang, W., Dong, C., Lin, J., Lin, Z., Cao, J.: Nucl. Fusion **57**, 126011 (2017)

12. Lin, Z., Hahm, T.S., Lee, W.W., Tang, W.M., White, R.B.: Turbulent transport reduction by zonal flows: massively parallel simulations. Science **281**, 1835 (1998)
13. http://phoenix.ps.uci.edu/GTC
14. http://www.iter.org
15. Lin, Z., Holod, I., Chen, L., Diamond, P.H., Hahm, T.S., Ethier, S.: Phys. Rev. Lett. **99**, 265003 (2007)
16. Xiao, Y., Lin, Z.: Turbulent transport of trapped electron modes in collisionless plasmas. Phys. Rev. Lett. **103**, 085004 (2009)
17. Zhang, W., Lin, Z., Chen, L.: Phys. Rev. Lett. **101**, 095001 (2008)
18. Zhang, W., Decyk, V., Holod, I., Xiao, Y., Lin, Z., Chen, L.: Phys. Plasmas **17**, 055902 (2010)
19. Zhang, W., Holod, I., Lin, Z., Xiao, Y.: Phys. Plasmas **19**, 022507 (2012)
20. Zhang, C., Zhang, W., Lin, Z., Li, D.: Phys. Plasmas **20**, 052501 (2013)
21. Wang, Z., et al.: Radial localization of toroidicity-induced alfven eigenmodes. Phys. Rev. Lett. **111**, 145003 (2013)
22. Cheng, J., et al.: Phys. Plasmas **23**, 052504 (2016)
23. Kuley, A., et al.: Phys. Plasmas **22**, 102515 (2015)
24. Peng, J., Zhihong, L., Holod, I., Chijie, X.: Plasma Sci. Technol **18**, 126 (2016)
25. McClenaghan, J., Lin, Z., Holod, I., Deng, W., Wang, Z.: Phys. Plasmas **21**, 122519 (2014)
26. Liu, D., Zhang, W., McClenaghan, J., Wang, J., Lin, Z.: Phys. Plasmas **21**, 122520 (2014)
27. Lin, Z., Hahm, T.S., Ethier, S., Tang, W.M.: Size scaling of turbulent transport in magnetically confined plasmas. Phys. Rev. Lett. **88**, 195004 (2002)
28. Meng, X., et al.: Heterogeneous programming and optimization of gyrokinetic toroidal code and large-scale performance test on TH-1A. In: Kunkel, J.M., Ludwig, T., Meuer, H.W. (eds.) ISC 2013. LNCS, vol. 7905, pp. 81–96. Springer, Heidelberg (2013). https://doi.org/10.1007/978-3-642-38750-0_7
29. Wang, E., et al.: The gyrokinetic particle simulation of fusion plasmas on Tianhe-2 supercomputer. In: Workshop on Latest Advances in Scalable Algorithms for Large-Scale Systems (ScalA) 2016, International Conference for High Performance Computing, Networking, Storage and Analysis (SC2016), Salt Lake City, USA (2016)
30. Madduri, K., et al.: Gyrokinetic toroidal simulations on leading multi- and manycore HPC systems. In: Proceedings of International Conference on High Performance Computing, Networking, Storage and Analysis, SC 2011 (2011)
31. Madduri, K., Im, E.J., Ibrahim, K.Z., Williams, S., Ethier, S., Oliker, L.: Gyrokinetic particle-in-cell optimization on emerging multi- and manycore platforms. Parallel Comput. **37**(9), 501–520 (2011)
32. Wang, B., et al.: Kinetic turbulence simulations at extreme scale on leadership-class systems. In: Proceedings of International Conference on High Performance Computing, Networking, Storage and Analysis, SC 2013, no. 82 (2013)
33. Ethier, S., Adams, M., Carter, J., Oliker, L.: Petascale parallelization of the gyrokinetic toroidal Code. LBNL Paper LBNL-4698 (2012)
34. Tang, W., Wang, B., Ethier, S.: Scientific discovery in fusion plasma turbulence simulations at extreme scale. Comput. Sci. Eng. **16**, 44 (2014)
35. Dawson, J.M.: Rev. Mod. Phys. **55**, 403 (1983)
36. Birdsall, C.K., Langdon, A.B.: Plasma Physics via Computer Simulation. CRC Press, Boca Raton (2004)
37. Xiao, Y., Holod, I., Wang, Z., Lin, Z., Zhang, T.: Phys. Plasmas **22**, 022516 (2015)
38. Feng, H., et al.: Development of finite element field solver in gyrokinetic toroidal code. Commun. Comput. Phys. **24**, 655 (2018)

39. Ethier, S., Lin, Z.: Porting the 3D gyrokinetic particle-in-cell code GTC to the NEC SX-6 vector architecture: perspectives and challenges. Comput. Phys. Commun. **164**, 456–458 (2004)

40. White, R.B., Chance, M.S.: Phys. Fluids **27**, 2455 (1984)

41. Joubert, W., et al.: Accelerated application development: the ORNL Titan experience. Comput. Electr. Eng. **46**, 123–138 (2015)

42. Vergara Larrea, V.G., et al.: Experiences evaluating functionality and performance of IBM POWER8+ systems. In: Kunkel, J.M., Yokota, R., Taufer, M., Shalf, J. (eds.) ISC High Performance 2017. LNCS, vol. 10524, pp. 254–274. Springer, Cham (2017). https://doi.org/10.1007/978-3-319-67630-2_20

Using Compiler Directives
for Performance Portability in Scientific
Computing: Kernels from Molecular
Simulation

Ada Sedova(✉)⬭, Andreas F. Tillack⬭, and Arnold Tharrington⬭

Scientific Computing Group, National Center for Computational Sciences,
Oak Ridge National Laboratory, Oak Ridge, TN 37830, USA
{sedovaaa,tillackaf,arnoldt}@ornl.gov

Abstract. Achieving performance portability for high-performance computing (HPC) applications in scientific fields has become an increasingly important initiative due to large differences in emerging supercomputer architectures. Here we test some key kernels from molecular dynamics (MD) to determine whether the use of the OpenACC directive-based programming model when applied to these kernels can result in performance within an acceptable range for these types of programs in the HPC setting. We find that for easily parallelizable kernels, performance on the GPU remains within this range. On the CPU, OpenACC-parallelized pairwise distance kernels would not meet the performance standards required, when using AMD Opteron "Interlagos" processors, but with IBM Power 9 processors, performance remains within an acceptable range for small batch sizes. These kernels provide a test for achieving performance portability with compiler directives for problems with memory-intensive components as are often found in scientific applications.

Keywords: Performance portability · OpenACC ·
Compiler directives · Pairwise distance · Molecular simulation

1 Introduction

Software development productivity is reduced when sections of high-performing programs must be frequently rewritten in low-level languages for new supercomputer architectures. This is not only a consequence of increased labor costs,

This manuscript has been authored by UT-Battelle, LLC under Contract No. DE-AC05-00OR22725 with the U.S. Department of Energy. The United States Government retains and the publisher, by accepting the article for publication, acknowledges that the United States Government retains a non-exclusive, paid-up, irrevocable, world-wide license to publish or reproduce the published form of this manuscript, or allow others to do so, for United States Government purposes. The Department of Energy will provide public access to these results of federally sponsored research in accordance with the DOE Public Access Plan (http://energy.gov/downloads/doe-public-access-plan).

S. Chandrasekaran et al. (Eds.): WACCPD 2018 Workshop, LNCS 11381, pp. 22–47, 2019.
https://doi.org/10.1007/978-3-030-12274-4_2

but also because the code can become more error-prone due to shortened life-times, multiple authors, and the inherent difficulty of programming close to machine-level [23,55,68,77]. Because of such considerations, creating performance portable applications has become an important effort in scientific computing [47,51], and is recognized as a significant software design goal by both the U.S. Department of Energy (DOE) [1,47,51] and the National Science Foundation (NSF) [15].

Classical molecular dynamics (MD) simulation is a popular tool for a number of fields within the physical and chemical sciences [30,69] and has been successfully implemented in the high-performance computing (HPC) setting by several developers [19,25,26,36,46,61,62,67,73]. The associated reports pay testimony to the extensive effort involved in porting these programs to different HPC platforms in order to meet increasingly rising standards. A variety of non-portable components are employed in leadership MD programs that allow for cutting-edge performance to be obtained. Some of the most performance-enhancing elements for per-node speedup include the CUDA C language (and CUDA API) for GPU-based acceleration, and architecture-specific SIMD intrinsic functions along with threading for the CPU portions [2–4,19,62,66,73]. CUDA C and the CUDA API, for example, are currently usable only with NVIDIA GPUs, so sections of code written in CUDA will have to be rewritten or translated for use on a different GPU-vendor's product; AMD GPUs, for instance, have recently been shown to be competitive to NVIDIA GPUs [35,75]. For optimal performance on CPU-portions of heterogeneous architectures, architecture-specific SIMD instructions implemented with either intrinsic functions or vector instructions are often found to be essential in leadership MD programs [58]: without the use of SIMD, a majority of the processor's capacity may be unused by a program, and many compilers are not effective in auto-vectorizing code [40], but highly optimized SIMD instructions are architecture-specific and require a considerable effort. This amount of effort may not be optimal or even permissible for a domain scientist, as it will detract from time spent in scientific pursuits. Nevertheless, scientific computing needs can often be very niche-specific and thus commercial applications may not provide an adequate computational solution [57]. Modern science has advanced to a level that some amount of computing is required for both the theoretical and experimental branches: while computational science has become recognized as the "third pillar" of science by national agencies such as the NSF [13], current trends indicate that it is now essential to the functioning of the other two [76]. It is thus of great importance that scientific computing initiatives have accessible programming tools to produce efficient code that can be easily ported to a number of HPC architectures, and that the machine-level back ends are re-targeted and optimized by system or API developers, while maintaining a consistent, unified front-end interface for the computational scientist to use.

High level, compiler-directive based programing models such as OpenACC and OpenMP have the potential to be used as a tool to create more performance portable code [16,17]. Results of such attempts have been mixed, however [28,31,47,48,51,56]. The creation of a dedicated portable program should provide the most optimal results [55,68]. Accordingly, here we test the possibility of creating a portable MD application starting with key kernels of the basic algorithm, and acceleration using OpenACC, to assess whether the resulting performance of these kernels is within an acceptable range to be used as part of HPC-based MD programs. This effort provides tests of the performance of OpenACC on kernels that involve non-negligible memory operations, and large memory transfers to the GPU, characteristic of many scientific applications. The kernels also represent calculations important to other types of computational work such as classification and data analysis.

2   Background

2.1   Performance Portability

To quantify portability, an index has been proposed, the degree of portability (DP):

$$DP = 1 - (C_P/C_R) \tag{1}$$

where C_P is the cost to port and C_R is the cost to rewrite the program [54]. Thus, a completely portable application has an index of one, and a positive index indicates that porting is more profitable. There are several types of portability; binary portability is the ability of the compiled code to run on a different machine, and source portability is the ability of the source code to be compiled on a different machine and then executed [54,55,68]. Here, costs can include development time and personnel compensations, as well as error production, reductions in efficiency or functionality, and even less tangible costs such as worker stress or loss of resources for other projects. For the HPC context, we can say that an application is performance portable if it is not only source-portable to a variety of HPC architectures using the Linux operating system and commonly provided compilers, but also that its performance remains in an acceptable range to be usable by domain scientists for competitive research. To avoid the ambiguity in the phrase "acceptable range," Pennycook and coworkers proposed the following metric for PP [45,60]:

$$PP(a, p, H) = \begin{cases} \frac{|H|}{\sum_{i \in H} \frac{1}{e_i(a,p)}} & \text{if } a \text{ is supported } \forall i \in H \\ 0 & \text{otherwise,} \end{cases} \tag{2}$$

where $|H|$ is the cardinality of the set H of all systems used to test the application a, p are the parameters used in a, and e_i is the efficiency of the application on each system $i \in H$. Efficiency, here, can be the ratio of performance of the given application to either the best-observed performance, or the peak theoretical hardware performance [60].

Use of a high-level programming interface with a re-targetable back end that is standardized and supported by a number of both commercial and open-source initiatives has been found to be a critical element of portable application design

[54,55]. OpenACC [16] was first developed to provide a high-level programming model for GPU programming, and now has been extended to multi-core machines. Conversely, OpenMP [17], once specific to CPU-based threading, has now been extended to the GPU. Both of these APIs offer compiler-directive-based interfaces with which to wrap sections of code for parallelization; they both appear in a similar format to the syntax used by OpenMP, which has now become familiar to many programmers of all levels. These two APIs are supported by a number of commercial hardware and compiler developers, and in addition, by the GNU project [18].

2.2 Molecular Dynamics

In molecular dynamics, a system, represented by atomistic units, is propagated in time based on some calculated forces using a numerical integration of Newton's equations of motion. The simulation cannot proceed with the next step until the previous one is completed; furthermore, a very small time-step is required to keep the simulation from sustaining unacceptable drifts in energy, as compared to experimental timescales that the simulation may be modeling [69]. Therefore, minimization of time per step is highly important. Several open-source, highly parallel classical MD programs exist that can scale to over thousands of nodes of a supercomputer and are heavily used internationally for molecular research. These programs are able to perform a time step in less than two milliseconds for systems of hundreds of thousands of atoms, or in seconds for systems of hundreds of millions of atoms [19,36,46,62,67,73].

The classical molecular dynamics algorithm involves three main components: the integration step, the calculation of bonded forces, of pairwise short-range non-bonded (SNF) forces, and the calculation of long-range forces. The integration step is generally the quickest part of the calculation, and as it has some memory-intensive aspects, is often calculated using the CPU, in implementations using heterogeneous architectures. The long-range forces calculation, in most implementations, involves an Ewald-sum, and requires Fourier transforms. The SNFs consist of the Lennard-Jones interaction, and short-range electrostatic forces. The Lennard-Jones interaction is an empirical function created to approximate the dispersive, or van der Waals forces, which in reality are purely quantum effects. The functional forms for these two additive forces are:

$$F_{LJ}(\mathbf{r_{ij}}) = \left[12\left(\frac{\sigma_{ij}^{12}}{r_{ij}^{13}}\right) - 6\left(\frac{\sigma_{ij}^6}{r_{ij}^7}\right) \right] \frac{\mathbf{r}_{ij}}{r_{ij}}, \tag{3}$$

$$F_C(\mathbf{r_{ij}}) = \frac{1}{4\pi\epsilon_0} \frac{q_i q_j}{r_{ij}^2} \frac{\mathbf{r}_{ij}}{r_{ij}}. \tag{4}$$

Here $F_{LJ}(\mathbf{r_{ij}})$ is the Lennard-Jones force on atom i due to atom j, with $\mathbf{r_{ij}}$ being the vector connecting atom i to atom j. σ is a parameter that depends on the atom type of both interacting atoms, and $F_C(\mathbf{r_{ij}})$ is the analogous Coulomb force, with q_n being the point-charge value assigned to atom n, and ϵ_0 the permittivity of free space; both are functions of the inter-atomic distance [5,69].

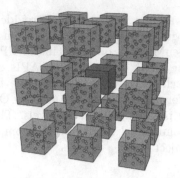

Fig. 1. Schematic of the interaction neighbors for cell-cell interactions involved in the spatial decomposition in the molecular dynamics algorithm. The central box (orange), interacts with itself, and with its 26 immediate neighbors, creating a total of 27 interactions for each cell in the grid, if in a periodic system, or a range of interactions from 8–27 if in a non-periodic system. Boxes are exploded outward for visualization purposes, but sides are touching in the actual grid. (Color figure online)

The Lennard-Jones and short-range electrostatic forces rapidly decay to zero outside of a radius of about 10–14 angstroms. This creates an excellent mechanism for reducing the total calculation by imposing a distance-based radial cutoff on each atom, outside of which no interactions are considered. Algorithmically, the SNF calculation usually consists of a spatial decomposition, or domain

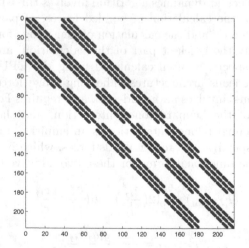

Fig. 2. Sparsity plot of distance matrix of all cell-cell distances, with all distances outside of radial cut-off of 10 angstroms set to zeros (and colored white), for a solvated system of 30,000 atoms (small protein), and all distances within the cut-off in blue. The number of cells in each direction is 6, resulting in a total of 46,656 cell-cell distances. 4096 of these are actually calculated in a non-periodic MD simulation due to the cut-off scheme. (Color figure online)

decomposition, of the system, into a three-dimensional grid of cells, followed by a binning of the atoms into their associated cells with some sort of sorting procedure. After this the pairwise forces on each atom can be calculated and summed [58,65]. These forces, as can be seen from their equations, depend on the pairwise distances between an atom and all other atoms within the radial cut-off. If the spatial decomposition is performed so that the cells' dimensions are close to the LJ cut-off distance, then only the interacting cell-cell pairs need to be searched for interacting atoms, for each cell [65]. In the periodic regime, all cells have 26 neighbors, and distances of all atoms within the central cell must be calculated as well, resulting in 27 cell-cell interactions that must be calculated for each cell in the grid of the domain decomposition. Figure 1 shows a central cell and its interacting cell neighbors. Figure 2 shows a sparsity plot of the distance matrix for all cell-cell interactions in the system, with those having distances greater than the cut-off set to zero and colored white, and interacting cells colored blue. As can be seen, the cut-off creates a banded structure to the matrix, and reduces the number of cell-cell calculations by about 90%.

3   Portability Goals: Timings and Architectures

HPC MD developers have continuously pushed for increasingly shorter per-time-step execution rates. Currently, GROMACS [19] and NAMD [73] exhibit highly competitive timings per time-step. For 21 M atoms, NAMD attained about 5 ms per time-step and for a 224 M atom system, about 40 ms per time-step using 4096 nodes, according to published benchmarks [6,63]. In 2015 GROMACS reported a sub-millisecond time-step for a 80,000 atom system using only 32 nodes, with Intel E5-2680v2 processors with 20 CPU cores and 2 K20X NVIDIA GPUs, and 1.7 ms per step for a 2 M atom system using 512 nodes of the same processor type but without GPU [46]; thus performance on a multi-core machine can actually exceed that of a GPU-enabled supercomputer for MD. Using GROMACS 5.1.3 on OLCF Titan, a Cray XK7 with AMD Interlagos CPUs and one NVIDIA K20X GPU per node we obtained a 1.2 ms time-step for a 1.1 M atom system using 1024 nodes. This level of performance has been attained and is expected on many-core, multi-core, *and* GPU-containing HPC systems.

We test some key kernels from a MD calculation to see if parallelization with OpenACC can be performed while remaining under 7 ms/time-step for a system under 20 M atoms, or 55 ms/time-step for a system of about 220 M atoms, after domain decomposition. On a single node, the total times for the kernels must be well below these numbers while at the same time the job size on the node must be large enough so that the total domain decomposition would not use more that about 2000 nodes for a smaller system, and 4000 nodes for a larger system. Common domain decomposition for MD programs involves computing the SNFs acting on about 15 K atoms on a single node. For around 15 K atoms, there are about 3,000 cell-cell interactions, so what we aim for is a total kernel time under 6 ms for about 3,000 cell-cell interactions, or 50 ms for about 12,000 cell-cell interactions, which leaves time for communication and other less time-consuming portions of the calculation, and corresponds to an 80% efficiency score compared to NAMD, and if maintained for all architectures tested, would result in a minimum of 80% performance portability score in (2). We test whether this performance can be maintained using the same source code, on nodes with multi-core CPUs and on heterogeneous nodes containing a GPU.

4   Designing the Kernels

4.1   The Programming Model and Its Portable Subset

C enjoys native support on a variety of machines and is familiar to most programmers, furthermore, C++ functionality has been added for some compilers [32], but can be problematic [56]. We try to use only the portable subset of C and OpenACC. For C/C++, this means avoiding structures and classes, and programming elements that are difficult to parallelize with directives. While OpenMP provides SIMD constructs that enable machine-specific elements to be added to a parallel region, OpenACC does not contain syntax for such explicit targeting [29,43,51,59]. Additionally, it has been found that OpenACC threading on the CPU can be poor if the optimal organization of a particular kernel is not used, and that this re-organization for the CPU can decrease performance on the GPU [28]. We would like for parallel regions to not have to be rearranged with different constructs to obtain adequate performance on different architectures. We tried to use the simplest layouts as an initial test, with the hope that the design and modularity of the application could provide a large portion of the parallel performance gain. Although the format of directive-based parallelization with OpenMP and OpenACC initially seem similar, unfortunately the two APIs differ enough in how they must be used to obtain adequate parallelization, that they cannot be exchanged using simple macros. In many cases, different sections of nested loops require different arrangement of parallel clauses, and in some cases, the code region must be re-arranged when switching between APIs [64,74,78]. There are initiatives that are aimed at performing an automated translation from one to the other; this is a positive development as currently only several compilers support each interface [74]. To facilitate such a translation it will also be advantageous to use the simplest syntax for each parallel region.

4.2   Modular Format and Kernels

To create a modular format that can facilitate portability, deconstruction of the MD algorithm into its subtasks was performed. To simplify the algorithm we avoid the use of non-rectangular cells for the domain decomposition. Several highly optimized algorithms have been published that focused on the use of cells of varying complexity, [19,24]; these types of algorithms require more time to code, understand, and test, and thus are not a practical choice for a dedicated portability effort. We chose a rectangular grid, and once the grid is created, the location of each atom can very easily be calculated using a reduction over its three position coordinates. A one-digit address can be uniquely determined.

We focus on several computational modules that are repeated every time step. The creation of the cell-grid, based on the minimum and maximum values of the atomic positions along each dimension, and the cut-off radius given, is an example of a procedure that only needs to be calculated one time for a constant-volume simulation. This is also true for the creation of the interaction list for the cell-cell interactions. The first module that is repeated is "atom-binning." Involved in this task is the assignment of each atom to its corresponding cell, referred to here as the "cell-assign" procedure. Additional steps involve counting the number of atoms in each cell, and the filling of a data structure representing each cell with the appropriate atoms' coordinates, either with a gathering of all atoms belonging to it, or with a halo-exchange type operation after an initial sorting. Cell-assignment is a completely parallel task that is trivial to distribute and requires no redesign from an analogous serial algorithm. For the rest of the parallel binning algorithm, however, it is impossible to simply parallelize the counting and the permutation-array steps with a directive added to a serial implementation: the concept of counting and all-prefix-sums are dependent on the sequential programmatic progression. This is an excellent example of how the use of OpenACC in a naïve way to speed-up a serial algorithm can fail completely. An algorithm's serial version may require a complete restructuring in a parallel programming model.

Another module we tested is the squared pairwise-distance calculation. This module comprises a large portion of the force computation in MD, which is the largest bottleneck [27,38]. The decay of the force functions, however, makes the cut-off approximation both accurate and very computationally important; the cell-based spatial decomposition makes excellent use of this [65]. The large, cell-cell pairwise distances calculation (the pairwise distance of each atom in each cell with all other atoms in interacting cells) has a complexity of $O(N)$, where N is the total number of atoms being modeled, however the prefactor is very large. To obtain the pairwise distances, an element-wise square root must be applied.

The pairwise distance calculation is also important for numerous applications in statistics and data science. A pairwise-distance calculation over a large number of multi-dimensional observations is central to clustering algorithms such as k-means and some kernel methods [21,41,49,70,71]. Therefore an analysis of the potential for performance portability of a massively parallel distance matrix calculator is of interest in its own right [20,49].

Many MD programs also employ an atomic neighbor-list, which not updated every time step under the assumption that the atoms will not move considerably each step. This reduces the number of times the pairwise distances within the cell interactions are calculated, thus it reduces the prefactor in the $O(N)$ complexity. However, this procedure incurs some launch overhead, memory access, and communication costs: potential inefficiency of many small data-structure-accessing steps, increased bookkeeping requirements in the code, and the requirement to "batch" the calculations by hand on the GPU for efficiency, lead to increases in code complexity and thus potential error-generation, and decreases in portability. We did not address the neighbor-list calculation in this study.

5   Binning Module (Neighbor-List Updates): Bin-Assign, Bin-Count, and Bin Sorting

5.1   Bin-Assign, Bin-Count

Listing 1.1 shows a serial version of the bin-assign and bin-counting procedures. The most efficient method, in serial, is to use a one-dimensional array of atoms' bin IDs, and an accompanying array that keeps track of how many atoms in each bin. In a serial implementation, this bin-count can be accomplished in the same for-loop as the bin-assign.

```
1
2  /* after determining the number of bins based on the total system size
       and the cutoff, allocate the array that keeps track of how many
       atoms are in each bin:            */
3    bin_count=(int *calloc(numbins*sizeof(int));
4  // binning procedure:
5    for (b = 0; b < num_atoms; b++) {
6  // read each atom's 3 coordinates and calculate the value of the 3-
       digit
7  // address:
8      temp[0] = floor((coords[b][0]/range[0]-kbinx)*num_divx);
9      temp[1] = floor((coords[b][1]/range[1]-kbiny)*num_divy);
10     temp[2] = floor((coords[b][2]/range[2]-kbinz)*num_divz);
11 // find the 1-digit address of the atom
12     n= num_divy*num_divz*(temp[0])+num_divz*(temp[1])+(temp[2]);
13 // enter the 1-digit address into that atom's index in the bin_ids
       array:
14     bin_ids[b] = n;
15 // update the count in that bin's index in the bin_count array:
16     bin_count[n]=bin_count[n]+1;
17   }
18 /* The variable bin_ids is a one-dimensional array the length of the
       number the total number of atoms. Each element of bins contains
       the single-integer bin ID of the atom with corresponding array
       index, and the variable coords is a two-dimensional array
       allocated at the initialization of the program, containing the x,
       y, and z components of each atom's coordinates. The variable
       bin_count is a tally of the number of elements in each bin. */
```

Listing 1.1. Code snippet of a serial version of bin-assign/bin-count

For a parallel version, "counting" is ill-defined, and this seemingly trivial computation in serial, becomes a more difficult task in parallel. The serial version of the gathering step is also relatively trivial. Listing 1.2 shows a version of this type of nested solution in a serial implementation.

```
1  count = 0;
2    for(b=0; b<numbins; b++) {
3      for(c=0; c<num_atoms; c++) {
4        if(bin_ids[c]==b){
5        gather_array[count]=c;
6        count++;
7        }
8      }
9    }
```

Listing 1.2. Code snippet of a serial version of the gathering array generation

Since the bin-assign procedure is independent for each atom, it is easily parallelizable. The requirements simply involve using a single OpenACC directive to parallelize the serial version. Listing 1.3 shows the implementation of its parallelization using an OpenACC parallel loop pragma. It is further possible to potentially optimize this section using different OpenACC options, however, with just this simple addition, using the PGI compiler, OpenACC generates an implicit copy_out of bin_ids, an implicit copy_in of coords and range. For 500,000 atoms, this section of the binning algorithm required 115 μs (0.115 ms), and for 30,000 atoms, 11 μs (0.011 ms), using one node of Titan with the GPU. Although the use of gangs, workers, and other data distribution keywords provided by OpenACC are defined for particular divisions of tasks, the actual performance of these various methods to create compiler-written code for a particular HPC architecture is highly system dependent. We found for the above kernel, that these additional constructs did not improve performance. The most general pragma, the "kernels" directive, allows the API to determine what regions of the section can be parallelized, and to distribute these regions appropriately. A less general option is the parallel "loop" region, which specifically tells the compiler to parallelize the loop.

```
#pragma acc parallel loop private(temp)
for (b = 0; b < num_atoms; b++) {
// read each atom's 3 coordinates and calculate the value of the 3-
      digit
// address:
  temp[0] = floor((coords[b][0]/range[0]-kbinx)*num_divx);
  temp[1] = floor((coords[b][1]/range[1]-kbiny)*num_divy);
  temp[2] = floor((coords[b][2]/range[2]-kbinz)*num_divz);
// find the 1-digit address of the atom
  bin_ids[b]= num_divy*num_divz*(temp[0])+num_divz*(temp[1])+(temp[2]);
}
```

Listing 1.3. Code snippet of a simple OpenAcc parallelization of bin-assign

Manual Task Division for Bin-Assign Together with OpenACC Pragmas. We also tested how some amount of manual splitting of the bin-assignment tasks would affect the speed-up. We separated the atoms into 5 evenly distributed blocks, and added OpenACC loops around both the blocks, and the inner bin-assign. Interestingly, this resulted in a 3−5 × speed-up, depending on the number of atoms. However, the speed-up may be system- and data-size-dependent, and it may be a difficult task to optimize this manual splitting by future users of the application.

5.2 Parallel Algorithm Design for Bin Count and Gather

The bin count and gather operations are classical examples of more difficult problems in parallel computing. For this reason, for a portable application, these modules may be better handled with optimized routines from libraries rather than OpenACC. Furthermore, the optimal programmatic solution may vary greatly between architectures. Details are provided below.

Bin Count. Parallelization of the bin-count procedure can be approached in several ways. This is ultimately a histogramming task. One can use an atomic-add for the bin-count array variable, which can be kept in a shared location in memory. These types of operations are supported by OpenACC's more advanced directive options. Alternately, one can create a type of merge-count, so that the bin-ID array is split into subarrays, each is counted in serial by parallel gangs, and the results are merged. It is also possible that for various architectures, there will be a different optimal solution for this step. Thus this is an example of a region of code that may require encapsulation and increased documentation, as well as several kernels to be used for specific systems, or the potential for exchanging with an optimized library. A high performing histogram routine, for instance, could be employed in this section [53], as can a parallel prefix-sum routine [39].

Gather. In order to gather all atomic coordinates belonging to a cell (bin) into a single data structure for passing to the pairwise distance calculation, the use of masks, or an efficient parallel scan algorithm can be used. This process involves a (fuzzy) sorting and somewhat complicated data movement patterns. The optimal solution can require a significant amount of effort and may vary greatly based on the architecture targeted, and thus is the type of procedure that could also be replaced with a call to hardware-specific libraries, that would each provide an optimized solution for a specific architecture. One possibility is to exploit sorting procedures provided by HPC libraries such as Thrust [7]. This again is a region that must be encapsulated and well-documented, because it may involve machine-specific solutions [33].

```
1  for(b=0; b<num_batch; b++){
2    /* rows=dim, columns=obs. */
3    for (i = 0; i < num_coords_n; i++) {
4      for (j = 0; j < num_coords_m; j++) {
5        for (k = 0; k < 3; k++)
6        {
7          temp =  batchA[b][k + 3 * i] - batchB[b][k + 3 * j];
8          y[k] = temp * temp;
9        }
10       temp = y[0];
11       for (k = 0; k < 2; k++)
12       {
13         temp += y[k + 1];
14       }
15       batchC[b][i + num_coords_n * j] = temp;
16     }
17   }
18 }
```

Listing 1.4. Code snippet of serial version of the squared pairwise distance calculation

After the initial gathering of atoms into their respective cell arrays, future gathering operations can be accomplished with a data exchange routine common in the halo-exchange algorithms used in stencil computations [22,37]. This takes advantage of the fact that atoms do not move large amounts over short time periods, and thus many atoms may not change cells for many time steps. Therefore the number of exchangers will be small. However, this approach involves communication expense and more complicated data movement patterns. Alternately, larger groups of atoms in neighboring cells can again be sorted by bin ID using a fast sorting algorithm that is most efficient on heavily presorted data [42,44,72]. For smaller systems where data is located on a single node, it may be faster to resort all atoms than to perform numerous communication and data exchange operations. Ultimately, the optimal choice of algorithm may also be hardware specific, and thus it is possible that the most performance portable solution for this module is a call to an HPC library.

6   The Squared Pairwise Distance Calculation: Performance, Portability, and Effort

In this section we examine the performance portability of an OpenACC implementation of the calculation of the squared pairwise distance matrix for all atoms in sets of two interacting cells. This calculation does not suffer from the types of algorithmic complexities that the bin count and gather modules do; it is a more easily parallelizable routine much like the bin assign module. For this module, in addition to the use of OpenACC for parallelization on the GPU and on the CPU, we also created two alternate implementations, one using a CUDA kernel, to compare performance of the directive-based implementation, and one completely using routines from newly emerging batched versions of accelerator-based Basic Linear Algebra Subprograms (BLAS) [12] libraries.

The BLAS version is a pedagogical example of a solution that is not only portable, but actually requires the least amount of parallel programming experience: it allows the user to perform the calculation without any knowledge of accelerator programming or even any experience with compiler directives. Thus the effort and skill required to port this version would be minimal. While batched versions of BLAS standard routines are not technically part of the standard, there is a growing need for these types of routines and they are available in many scientific libraries.

Listing 1.4 shows the serial version of such a calculation. The variables batchA and batchB are batched collections of atoms in interacting cells, batchC is an array of respective distance matrices for each cell pair from in batchA and batchB, and num_cells is the number of cells in each batch. There is a loop over the three dimensions in order to provide generality: for use in data analysis the dimension may be very large and parallelization of the loop may be necessary.

We tested single node, single GPU and CPU-only implementations, implementing parallelization with OpenACC, CUDA and cuBLAS using OLCF Titan, a Cray XK7 with 16-core AMD Opteron "Interlagos" CPUs and NVIDIA Kepler (K20X) GPUS, and OLCF Summit, a system containing 42 IBM POWER9 CPUs and 6 NVIDIA Volta (V100) GPUs per node, with 4 SMT hardware threads per CPU core [8].

```
 1 #pragma acc data copyin(A[0:3*num_batch*num_coords_n]),copyin(B[0:3*
     num_batch*num_coords_m])
 2
 3 pairwise_batched(A, B, C, num_coords_n, num_coords_m, num_batch);
 4
 5 void pairwise_batched(double A[], double B[], double C[], int ldX, int
     ldY, int num_batch){
 6 #pragma acc data present(A), present(B), present(C)
 7 #pragma acc kernels
 8 #pragma acc loop independent
 9   for (int b=0; b<num_batch; b++)
10   {
11     double y[3];
12     double temp;
13     /* rows=dim, columns=obs. */
14 #pragma acc loop independent
15     for (int i = 0; i < ldX; i++) {
16 #pragma acc loop independent
17       for (int j = 0; j < ldY; j++) {
18 #pragma acc loop seq
19        for (int k = 0; k < 3; k++)
20        {
21          double temp =  A[b*3*ldX + k + 3 * i] - B[b*3*ldY + k + 3 *
     j];
22          y[k] = temp * temp;
23        }
24        temp = y[0];
25 #pragma acc loop seq
26        for (int k = 0; k < 2; k++)
27        {
28          temp += y[k + 1];
29        }
30        C[b*ldX*ldY + i + ldX * j] = temp;
31       }
32     }
33   }
34 }
```

Listing 1.5. Code snippet of a simple OpenACC parallelization of the squared pairwise distance calculation

6.1   Use of OpenACC for the Squared Distance Calculation: GPU

The GPU-based OpenACC version was created by adding a data region, an acc kernels region, and three acc loop independent regions around the serial pairwise distance function shown in Listing 1.4. The two dimensional array was also flattened. Listing 1.5 shows this implementation. While there may be further work to be done in determining the optimal OpenACC clauses to use for this calculation, for the scheme shown in Listing 1.5, results were surprisingly good. On both Titan and Summit, a reasonable number of batches could be processed in under 10 ms, and on Summit, all cell-cell interactions for a system the size of a small protein (about 6000 batches) could be processed on a single GPU in under 10 ms. Figure 3A shows timings for increasing batch sizes using one node and one GPU of each machine. These results are within the acceptable range we determined for an MD step, although for smaller systems the upper limit on the time-per-step greatly constrains the amount of batches that can be offloaded to a single node, resulting in the use of only a small percent of the peak FLOPs available on the GPU (Fig. 4A). With no such constraint, it would be possible to perform significantly more pairwise distance calculations per node in a relatively

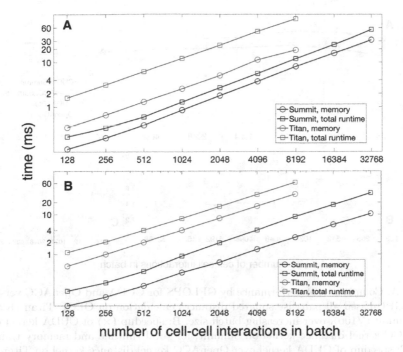

Fig. 3. Comparison of performance (time in ms), for CUDA and OpenACC versions of the GPU-based all-pairwise squared distances calculation on OLCF Titan (K20X) and Summit (V100), over increasing batch sizes. A: using OpenACC distance kernel. B: using CUDA distance kernel.

rapid amount of time based on how much the two tested GPUs' global memories can hold.

For larger systems, it may be advantageous to use more batches per node, and maximize the percentage of peak FLOPs used, as the amount of allowed time per time step for larger systems by current standard is higher. For a system of about 80,000 atoms, as in the GROMACS benchmark discussed in Sect. 3, using about 1024 batches per node, the distance calculation can be completed for all interacting atoms in under 10 ms using less than 8 nodes. Using 32 nodes, as used in the benchmark, this calculation can be completed in under 0.5 ms on Summit. Of course there are some additional calculations to be performed, i.e. the square root and the application of the force functions to the distances, to complete the SNF routine, however, these involve fewer FLOPs and no further memory transfers. The possibility of using OpenACC on GPUs within a performance-portable HPC MD application is not excluded by these initial benchmarks.

6.2 Comparison to CUDA Kernel

Figure 3B shows timings for the CUDA implementation of this calculation on Titan and Summit, and Fig. 4B-C shows speedup over the OpenACC version. Figure 5 shows memory transfer times.

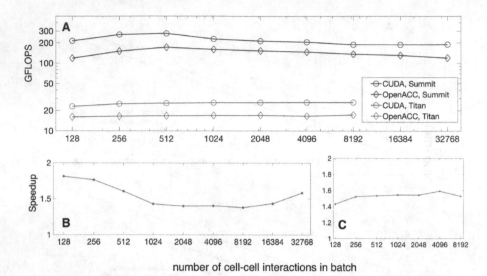

number of cell-cell interactions in batch

Fig. 4. A. Comparison of performance by GFLOPS for CUDA and OpenACC versions of the GPU-based all-pairwise squared distances calculation on OLCF Titan (K20X) and Summit (V100), over increasing batch size. B: speedup (×) of CUDA kernel over OpenACC kernel distance kernel on Summit, for total runtime and memory transfer time. C: speedup of CUDA kernel over OpenACC kernel distance kernel on Titan.

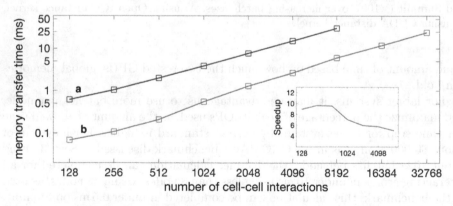

Fig. 5. Comparison of memory transfer time for CUDA versions (and BLAS version) of the GPU-based all-pairwise squared distances calculation on (a) OLCF Titan (K20X) and (b) Summit (V100), for different batch sizes. Inset: speedup (×) for Summit versus Titan

6.3   OpenACC on the CPU

We tested the parallelization of the kernel using OpenACC for CPU-based threading with the `ta=multicore` compiler flag, using the identical code. There are some algorithms that can be performed faster on the CPU, with OpenMP threading, than on the GPU with OpenACC or CUDA [9,46,64]. To get maximum performance on the CPU one must use threading, alignment, and vectorization [40], OpenACC has no functionality for intrinsic-function level specification. It also has no option for treating thread affinity. OpenACC seems to be less useful for creating truly performant CPU-based kernels than GPU version, for kernels like the distance calculation. Memory transfer time was sub-microsecond, and is not reported. Figure 6 shows kernel runtimes for varying batch sizes and scaling data on Summit and Titan. For smaller batch sizes, times can be within an acceptable range for Summit, but not Titan. Furthermore, the small batch size limit reduces the number of cell-cell interactions to those in an equivalent system of about 20,000 atoms. Therefore, we see that performance of OpenACC, even on new supercomputer cores, is barely within the lowest limit for performance portability.

6.4   Comparison to a Purely BLAS-Based Algorithm: Lowest Programming Knowledge Required

A well-known algorithm for the pairwise distance calculation can be implemented completely with subroutines from BLAS libraries. Surprisingly, although this algorithm involves slightly more total flops and a significant amount of memory operations than the direct method, it has been considered in the past as a fast way to implement the distance calculation on the CPU, if using threaded scientific libraries like Intel's MKL [49]. Matrix operations such as matrix-matrix multiplication are included in most high-performing scientific libraries provided by system manufacturers, and have also become benchmarks for measuring the performance of these systems. Thus they are competitively implemented in a highly optimized manner. The algorithm for the BLAS-based distance matrix calculation is shown in Algorithm 1.

The BLAS-based algorithm would probably be used on a single large matrix, in data analysis. Here we explored the potential of using such an algorithm on the GPU with a more recently developed massively-parallel extension of matrix-matrix multiplication (MM), the batched MM routines, to compare performance to our other two versions. While as-yet not a standard BLAS routine, a batched version of MM for many small matrices exits in both the NVIDIA provided cuBLAS library [10], and Intel MKL for multicore architectures and the KNL [14]. Furthermore, an version of a batched MM routine is provided by Magma, [11] an open-source effort that creates accelerated BLAS routines for a number of architectures. There is a growing possibility that batched BLAS routines

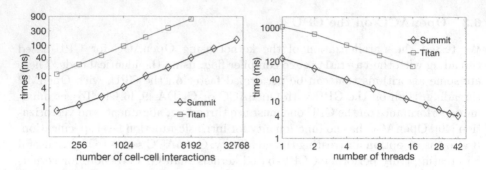

Fig. 6. Performance and scaling (time in ms) of OpenACC threading on the CPU, Summit and Titan, for all-pairwise squared distances calculation. Left: performance. Right: scaling plot for 1024 cell-cell interactions (batch number 1024).

will enter into the standard, as they arise naturally when large problems are decomposed on parallel platforms [34].

The BLAS method creates a floor for the amount of programming skill and effort required for an accelerated squared pairwise distance calculation. With this version programmer would not need to have any experience in any programming languages other than C/C++ or FORTRAN, not even the use of compiler directives. However, this algorithm works best for large matrices that are closer-to-square in shape, unlike our coordinate arrays.

Algorithm 1. Pairwise squared distance calculation using matrix operations, adapted form Li et al., 2011 [49]

1: load matrices $\mathbf{A}$ and $\mathbf{B}$ and allocate memory for matrix $\mathbf{C}$
2: $\mathbf{A}$ has dimension N by 3, $\mathbf{B}$ has dimension M by 3, and $\mathbf{C}$ has dimension N by M
3: note: $(\cdot)$ denotes elementwise multiplication
4: $\mathbf{v}_1 = (\mathbf{A} \cdot \mathbf{A})[1,1,1]^{\mathrm{T}}$
5: $\mathbf{v}_2 = (\mathbf{B} \cdot \mathbf{B})[1,1,1]^{\mathrm{T}}$
6: $\mathbf{P}_1 = [\mathbf{v}_1, \mathbf{v}_1, ..., \mathbf{v}_1]$ (dimension N by M)
7: $\mathbf{P}_2 = [\mathbf{v}_2, \mathbf{v}_2, ..., \mathbf{v}_2]^{\mathrm{T}}$ (dimension N by M)
8: $\mathbf{P}_3 = \mathbf{A}\mathbf{B}^{T}$ (dimension N by M)
9: $\mathbf{D}^2 = (\mathbf{P}_1 + \mathbf{P}_2 - 2\mathbf{P}_3)$, where $\mathbf{D}^2$ is the matrix of squared distances
10: pairwise distance matrix can be recovered from $\mathbf{D}^2$ by element-wise square-root

---

We implemented this algorithm using cuBLAS, the CUDA-based BLAS library provided by NVIDIA. Using matrices of size 200 by 3, we tested this implementation on a single GPU of Titan and Summit. Matrices $\mathbf{A}$ and $\mathbf{B}$ in our situation are the 3-D coordinates for atoms in two interacting cells. In order to perform lines 6 and 7 with BLAS routines, one can use the `dger` routine (outer product) of v_1 or v_2 with a vector of ones of length N. However, cuBLAS does not provide a batched version of `dger`, and thus we used batched MM again with input "matrices" v_1 or v_2 and a vector of ones. The element-wise multiplication is available in MKL as a Hadamard product, but not in cuBLAS, thus lines 4 and 5 were performed on the CPU and not included in timings. Because of this, we found that on the GPU, this algorithm cannot be performed completely with cuBLAS functions. Even without these first two components of the calculation, the performance of this method on the GPU compared to that of OpenACC or CUDA-C is much lower. Figures 7 and 8 show timings and comparison to the CUDA kernel. This (partial) version's performance is quite poor, but better than the OpenACC-threaded CPU version. Despite optimized BLAS routines on the GPU provided by NVIDIA, the memory operations swamp the performance in comparison to the CUDA-C and the GPU-based OpenACC versions.

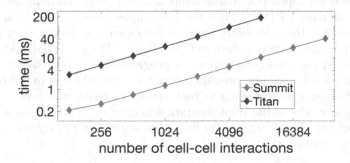

Fig. 7. Comparison of performance of BLAS version, all-pairwise squared distances calculation, on the GPU, using OLCF Titan (K20X) versus Summit (V100).

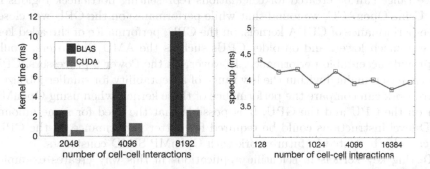

Fig. 8. Left: comparison of performance (time, ms) of BLAS versus CUDA version of all-pairwise squared distances calculation, using one GPU on Summit. Right: speedup (×) of CUDA version on Summit vs. cuBLAS-batched version on Summit.

7   Programming Effort

It is difficult to measure worker effort, especially when skill levels of workers may differ. Some papers report that CUDA requires more effort than OpenACC, even for workers familiar with both APIs [50,52,56]. However, different compilers each may implement a particular directive instruction differently, and variable performance may require alternate constructs to be used to parallelize a particular section of code, leading to some level of trial and error in each port. This lack of a defined outcome increases potentials for performance portability, as there are more possibilities that optimal performance will be obtained by using different constructs and different compilers, but can be frustrating for the user, and increased experience may not increase the ease of this process. Therefore, we cannot say that the use of OpenACC requires significantly less total worker effort than use of CUDA-C for small kernels. On the other hand, the amount effort required for OpenACC parallelization is not large, and the result is far more portable than CUDA-C after the first implementation has been created. It is also possible that the effort required for OpenACC is less than for some alternative portable solutions, such as OpenCL [52]. The use of cuBLAS-batched indeed required the minimum amount of programming skill, however, creating the kernel involved more programming steps than the addition of a directive to a serial kernel, and more testing to make sure the result was correct. On the other hand, after the initial implementation is created, it should be able to be used without any changes except for linking to a different library and any small changes to the call syntax.

8   Conclusions

We have found that portable kernels that remain within an acceptable performance range can be created for calculations representing bottleneck regions in MD. Using OpenACC, we found that while performance on the GPU was closer to the performance of CUDA kernels, on the CPU, performance of threaded kernels was much lower, and on older CPUs such as the AMD Bulldozers, would not provide acceptable performance. However, on the Power 9 processors, CPU performance remained within the low range of acceptability for smaller job sizes. Future work can compare the performance of these kernels when using OpenMP both on the CPU and the GPU. It is possible that the need for some amount SIMD-level instructions could be required for better performance on the CPU, and can also be tested in future work with OpenMP SIMD constructs.

Testing key kernels in scientific applications in this way creates examples of directive-based parallelization that include memory-limited calculations and difficult-to-parallelize algorithms, and expose routines that may perform in a less-than-efficient way. These examples, in turn, give the API developers test problems that may be outside of their usual testing routines, and thus help to maintain the cycle of collaboration between computational scientists and API developers that is seen as a requirement for the creation of portable, high-level interfaces for applications.

Challenges presented by the designing of HPC-portable applications using compiler directives include difficulties in the creation of parallel versions from serial routines, and can reveal the need for the use of high-performance libraries created for each particular architecture by specialists for certain encapsulated sections, instead of using the directives in those regions. It is possible that through the use of carefully designed modules and functions, together with directive-based programming models such as OpenACC, acceptable performance for some tasks can be achieved relatively easily. This can allow for a unified, performance portable interface for applications.

A   Artifact Description Appendix: Using Compiler Directives for Performance Portability in Scientific Computing: Kernels from Molecular Simulation

A.1   Abstract

This appendix details the run environments, compilers used, and compile line arguments for the four tested methods details in the text. Note that hardware access is limited to OLCF users.

A.2   Description

Check-list (artifact meta information)

- **Algorithm: Select kernels used in molecular dynamics**
- **Compilation: See compliers and commands below**
- **Binary: C++/CUDA or C++/OpenACC**
- **Run-time environment: Modules displayed below**
- **Hardware: OLCF Titan and Summit as described in main text**
- **Run-time state: Summit used SMT = 1 for CPU threading. Run commands below**
- **Execution: Run commands below, BLAS routines were called using standard calls to the cuBLAS library**
- **Publicly available?: All kernels are provided in the text and appendix**

All kernels used are listed in the main text, except the CUDA kernel. This is provided below:

```
template<typename T, int BS>
__global__ void
distance_kernel (T** A_data, T** B_data, T** C_data, int lda)
{
  int row_stride = lda;
  int row = blockIdx.x*BS+threadIdx.x;
  int col = blockIdx.y*BS+threadIdx.y;
  __shared__ T *A, *B, *C;
  if(threadIdx.x+threadIdx.y==0)
  {
    A = A_data[blockIdx.z];
```

```
12      B = B_data[blockIdx.z];
13      C = C_data[blockIdx.z];
14    }
15    __syncthreads();
16    if ((row < lda) && (col < lda))
17    {
18      T elementSum = (T)0.0;
19  #pragma unroll
20      for(int i=0; i<3; i++)
21      {
22        T diff = A[i*row_stride+row] - B[i*row_stride+col];
23        elementSum += diff*diff;
24      }
25      C[col * row_stride + row] = elementSum;
26    }
27  }
28  void
29  cuda_distance(double** A_data, double** B_data, double** C_data,
30                int lda, int numBatches)
31  {
32    const int BS = 16;
33    int NB = (lda+BS-1)/BS;
34    dim3 dimBlock(BS,BS);
35    dim3 dimGrid(NB,NB,numBatches);
36    distance_kernel<double,BS><<<dimGrid,dimBlock>>>
37    ((double**)A_data, (double**)B_data, (double**)C_data, lda);
38  }
```

Listing 1.6. CUDA version of batched pairwise distance calculation

Software Dependencies. Below are the modules, compilers, and run commands used.

```
1  CUDA/BLAS ON SUMMIT, MODULES:
2    gcc/5.4.0  cuda/9.1.85
3  CUDA/BLAS TITAN MODULES:
4    gcc/6.3.0 cudatoolkit/9.1.85_3.10-1.0502.df1cc54.3.1
5
6  Compiler calls
7  CPP = g++
8  CPPFLAGS = -Wall -O3
9  NVCC = nvcc
10 NVCCFLAGS = -arch=sm_35 -Drestrict=__restrict__ -DNO_CUDA_MAIN -O3
11
12 OPENACC, GPU VERSION:
13 COMPILER = pgc++
14 COMP_FLAGS = -acc -ta=nvidia:cc35 -Minfo=accel -mp
15 #replace with Summit version nvidia:cc70
16
17 SUMMIT EXECUTION:
18 jsrun --rs_per_host ${NPPNODE} --nrs ${NP} -ELD_LIBRARY_PATH -c7 -g1
      ./matrix_mul_batched > benchmark.SUMMIT.job
19 jsrun --rs_per_host ${NPPNODE} --nrs ${NP} -ELD_LIBRARY_PATH -c7 -g1
      ./directDist3 > ACC_benchmark.SUMMIT.job
20 }
21
22 Compiler output, Titan:
23 make pairwise_batched.o
24 make[1]: Entering directory
25 pgc++ -acc -ta=nvidia:cc35 -Minfo=accel -mp -c pairwise_batched.cpp -o
      pairwise_batched.o
26 pairwise_batched(double *, double *, double *, int, int, int):
27      4, Generating present(D[:],Y[:],X[:])
28      9, Loop is parallelizable
29        CUDA shared memory used for y
```

```
30       15, Loop is parallelizable
31       17, Loop is parallelizable
32           Accelerator kernel generated
33           Generating Tesla code
34            9, #pragma acc loop gang /* blockIdx.z */
35           15, #pragma acc loop gang, vector(128) /* blockIdx.x
      threadIdx.x */
36           17, #pragma acc loop gang /* blockIdx.y */
37           19, #pragma acc loop seq
38           26, #pragma acc loop seq
39       19, Complex loop carried dependence of X->,y,Y-> prevents
         parallelization
40 make[1]: Leaving directory '/autofs/nccs-svm1_home1/andreas/sources/
      D2Calc/AT/ACC'
41 pgc++ -acc -ta=nvidia:cc35 -Minfo=accel -mp -o directDist3 directDist3
      .cpp pairwise_batched.o
42 directDist3.cpp:
43 main:
44       43, Generating copy(D[:batch_count*40000])
45       61, Generating copyin(T[:batch_count*600],U[:batch_count*600])
46       73, Generating copyin(U[:batch_count*600],T[:batch_count*600])
47
48 Compiler output, Summit: Identical
49
50 OPENACC, CPU VERSION:
51 COMPILER = pgc++
52 COMP_FLAGS = -acc -ta=multicore -Minfo=accel -mp
```

Listing 1.7. Compile and run information

References

1. https://www.lanl.gov/asc/doe-coe-mtg-2017.php. Accessed 20 Aug 2018
2. https://gerrit.gromacs.org/. Accessed 22 Aug 2018
3. https://lammps.sandia.gov/. Accessed 20 Aug 2018
4. https://lammps.sandia.gov/doc/Speed/_intel.html. Accessed 27 Aug 2018
5. http://manual.gromacs.org/documentation/2016/manual-2016.pdf. Accessed 31 Aug 2018
6. www.ks.uiuc.edu/Research/namd/performance.html. Accessed 14 July 2017
7. thrust.github.io. Accessed 19 July 2017
8. https://www.olcf.ornl.gov/olcf-resources/. Accessed 6 Sept 2018
9. https://www.cp2k.org/performance. Accessed 27 Aug 2018
10. https://docs.nvidia.com/cuda/cublas/index.html. Accessed 24 Aug 2018
11. icl.cs.utk.edu/magma. Accessed 19 July 2017
12. BLAS (basic linear algebra subprograms). www.netlib.org/blas. Accessed 19 July 2017
13. Computational and data-enabled science and engineering. https://www.nsf.gov. Accessed 14 July 2017
14. Introducing batch GEMM operations. https://software.intel.com/en-us/articles/introducing-batch-gemm-operations. Accessed 6 Sept 2018
15. NSF/Intel partnership on computer assisted programming for heterogeneous architectures (CAPA). https://www.nsf.gov/funding/pgm_summ.jsp?pims_id=505319. Accessed 20 Aug 2018
16. www.openacc.org (2017). Accessed 14 July 2017
17. www.openmp.org (2017). Accessed 14 July 2017
18. www.gnu.org (2017). Accessed 14 July 2017

19. Abraham, M.J., et al.: GROMACS: high performance molecular simulations through multi-level parallelism from laptops to supercomputers. SoftwareX **1**, 19–25 (2015)

20. Al-Neama, M.W., Reda, N.M., Ghaleb, F.F.: An improved distance matrix computation algorithm for multicore clusters. BioMed Res. Int. **2014**, 1–12 (2014)

21. Arefin, A.S., Riveros, C., Berretta, R., Moscato, P.: Computing large-scale distance matrices on GPU. In: 2012 7th International Conference on Computer Science & Education (ICCSE), pp. 576–580. IEEE (2012)

22. Barrett, R.F., Vaughan, C.T., Heroux, M.A.: MiniGhost: a miniapp for exploring boundary exchange strategies using stencil computations in scientific parallel computing. Technical report. SAND 5294832, Sandia National Laboratories (2011)

23. Bonati, C., et al.: Design and optimization of a portable LQCD Monte Carlo code using OpenACC. Int. J. Mod. Phys. C **28**(05), 1750063 (2017)

24. Bowers, K.J., Dror, R.O., Shaw, D.E.: Zonal methods for the parallel execution of range-limited N-body simulations. J. Comput. Phys. **221**(1), 303–329 (2007)

25. Brown, W.M., Carrillo, J.M.Y., Gavhane, N., Thakkar, F.M., Plimpton, S.J.: Optimizing legacy molecular dynamics software with directive-based offload. Comput. Phys. Commun. **195**, 95–101 (2015)

26. Brown, W.M., Wang, P., Plimpton, S.J., Tharrington, A.N.: Implementing molecular dynamics on hybrid high performance computers-short range forces. Comput. Phys. Commun. **182**(4), 898–911 (2011)

27. Brown, W.M., Yamada, M.: Implementing molecular dynamics on hybrid high performance computers—three-body potentials. Comput. Phys. Commun. **184**(12), 2785–2793 (2013)

28. Calore, E., Gabbana, A., Kraus, J., Schifano, S.F., Tripiccione, R.: Performance and portability of accelerated lattice Boltzmann applications with OpenACC. Concurr. Comput. Pract. Exp. **28**(12), 3485–3502 (2016)

29. Chandrasekaran, S., Juckeland, G.: OpenACC for Programmers: Concepts and Strategies. Addison-Wesley Professional, Boston (2017)

30. Ciccotti, G., Ferrario, M., Schuette, C.: Molecular dynamics simulation. Entropy **16**, 233 (2014)

31. Codreanu, V., et al.: Evaluating automatically parallelized versions of the support vector machine. Concurr. Comput. Pract. Exp. **28**(7), 2274–2294 (2016)

32. PGI Compilers and Tools: OpenACC getting started guide. https://www.pgroup.com/resources/docs/18.5/pdf/openacc18_gs.pdf. Accessed 31 Aug 2018

33. Decyk, V.K., Singh, T.V.: Particle-in-cell algorithms for emerging computer architectures. Comput. Phys. Commun. **185**(3), 708–719 (2014)

34. Dongarra, J., Hammarling, S., Higham, N.J., Relton, S.D., Valero-Lara, P., Zounon, M.: The design and performance of batched blas on modern high-performance computing systems. Procedia Comput. Sci. **108**, 495–504 (2017)

35. Garvey, J.D., Abdelrahman, T.S.: A strategy for automatic performance tuning of stencil computations on GPUs. Sci. Programm. **2018**, 1–24 (2018)

36. Götz, A.W., Williamson, M.J., Xu, D., Poole, D., Le Grand, S., Walker, R.C.: Routine microsecond molecular dynamics simulations with AMBER on GPUs. 1. Generalized born. J. Chem. Theory Comput. **8**(5), 1542–1555 (2012)

37. Guo, X., Rogers, B.D., Lind, S., Stansby, P.K.: New massively parallel scheme for incompressible smoothed particle hydrodynamics (ISPH) for highly nonlinear and distorted flow. Comput. Phys. Commun. **233**, 16–28 (2018)

38. Hardy, D.J.: Improving NAMD performance on multi-GPU platforms. In: 16th Annual Workshop on Charm++ and its Applications. https://charm.cs.illinois.edu/workshops/charmWorkshop2018/slides/CharmWorkshop2018_namd_hardy.pdf (2018)
39. Harris, M., Sengupta, S., Owens, J.D.: Parallel prefix sum (scan) with CUDA, chapter 39. In: Nguyen, H. (ed.) GPU Gems 3. Addison-Wesley, Boston (2008)
40. Huber, J., Hernandez, O., Lopez, G.: Effective vectorization with OpenMP 4.5, ORNL/TM-2016/391. Technical report, Oak Ridge National Lab. (ORNL), Oak Ridge, TN (United States). Oak Ridge Leadership Computing Facility (OLCF) (2017)
41. Jain, A.K.: Data clustering: 50 years beyond K-means. Pattern Recogn. Lett. **31**(8), 651–666 (2010)
42. Jocksch, A., Hariri, F., Tran, T.-M., Brunner, S., Gheller, C., Villard, L.: A bucket sort algorithm for the particle-in-cell method on manycore architectures. In: Wyrzykowski, R., Deelman, E., Dongarra, J., Karczewski, K., Kitowski, J., Wiatr, K. (eds.) PPAM 2015. LNCS, vol. 9573, pp. 43–52. Springer, Cham (2016). https://doi.org/10.1007/978-3-319-32149-3_5
43. Juckeland, G., et al.: From describing to prescribing parallelism: translating the SPEC ACCEL OpenACC suite to OpenMP target directives. In: Taufer, M., Mohr, B., Kunkel, J.M. (eds.) ISC High Performance 2016. LNCS, vol. 9945, pp. 470–488. Springer, Cham (2016). https://doi.org/10.1007/978-3-319-46079-6_33
44. Kale, V., Solomonik, E.: Parallel sorting pattern. In: Proceedings of the 2010 Workshop on Parallel Programming Patterns, p. 10. ACM (2010)
45. Kirk, R.O., Mudalige, G.R., Reguly, I.Z., Wright, S.A., Martineau, M.J., Jarvis, S.A.: Achieving performance portability for a heat conduction solver mini-application on modern multi-core systems. In: 2017 IEEE International Conference on Cluster Computing (CLUSTER), pp. 834–841. IEEE (2017)
46. Kutzner, C., Páll, S., Fechner, M., Esztermann, A., de Groot, B.L., Grubmüller, H.: Best bang for your buck: GPU nodes for GROMACS biomolecular simulations. J. Comput. Chem. **36**(26), 1990–2008 (2015)
47. Larrea, V.V., Joubert, W., Lopez, M.G., Hernandez, O.: Early experiences writing performance portable OpenMP 4 codes. In: Proceedings of Cray User Group Meeting, London, England (2016)
48. Lashgar, A., Baniasadi, A.: Employing software-managed caches in OpenACC: opportunities and benefits. ACM Trans. Model. Perform. Eval. Comput. Syst. **1**(1), 2 (2016)
49. Li, Q., Kecman, V., Salman, R.: A chunking method for Euclidean distance matrix calculation on large dataset using multi-GPU. In: 2010 Ninth International Conference on Machine Learning and Applications (ICMLA), pp. 208–213. IEEE (2010)
50. Li, X., Shih, P.C., Overbey, J., Seals, C., Lim, A.: Comparing programmer productivity in OpenACC and CUDA: an empirical investigation. Int. J. Comput. Sci. Eng. Appl. (IJCSEA) **6**(5), 1–15 (2016)
51. Lopez, M.G., et al.: Towards achieving performance portability using directives for accelerators. In: 2016 Third Workshop on Accelerator Programming Using Directives (WACCPD), pp. 13–24. IEEE (2016)
52. Memeti, S., Li, L., Pllana, S., Kołodziej, J., Kessler, C.: Benchmarking OpenCL, OpenACC, OpenMP, and CUDA: programming productivity, performance, and energy consumption. In: Proceedings of the 2017 Workshop on Adaptive Resource Management and Scheduling for Cloud Computing, pp. 1–6. ACM (2017)

53. Milic, U., Gelado, I., Puzovic, N., Ramirez, A., Tomasevic, M.: Parallelizing general histogram application for CUDA architectures. In: 2013 International Conference on Embedded Computer Systems: Architectures, Modeling, and Simulation (SAMOS XIII), pp. 11–18. IEEE (2013)
54. Mooney, J.D.: Bringing portability to the software process. Department of Statistics and Computer Science, West Virginia University, Morgantown WV (1997)
55. Mooney, J.D.: Developing portable software. In: Reis, R. (ed.) Information Technology. IIFIP, vol. 157, pp. 55–84. Springer, Boston, MA (2004). https://doi.org/10.1007/1-4020-8159-6_3
56. Nicolini, M., Miller, J., Wienke, S., Schlottke-Lakemper, M., Meinke, M., Müller, M.S.: Software cost analysis of GPU-accelerated aeroacoustics simulations in C++ with OpenACC. In: Taufer, M., Mohr, B., Kunkel, J.M. (eds.) ISC High Performance 2016. LNCS, vol. 9945, pp. 524–543. Springer, Cham (2016). https://doi.org/10.1007/978-3-319-46079-6_36
57. Nori, R., Karodiya, N., Reza, H.: Portability testing of scientific computing software systems. In: 2013 IEEE International Conference on Electro/Information Technology (EIT), pp. 1–8. IEEE (2013)
58. Páll, S., Abraham, M.J., Kutzner, C., Hess, B., Lindahl, E.: Tackling exascale software challenges in molecular dynamics simulations with GROMACS. In: Markidis, S., Laure, E. (eds.) EASC 2014. LNCS, vol. 8759, pp. 3–27. Springer, Cham (2015). https://doi.org/10.1007/978-3-319-15976-8_1
59. Van der Pas, R., Stotzer, E., Terboven, C.: Using OpenMP–The Next Step: Affinity, Accelerators, Tasking, and SIMD. MIT Press, Cambridge (2017)
60. Pennycook, S.J., Sewall, J.D., Lee, V.: A metric for performance portability. arXiv preprint arXiv:1611.07409 (2016)
61. Phillips, J.C., et al.: Scalable molecular dynamics with namd. J. Comput. Chem. 26(16), 1781–1802 (2005)
62. Phillips, J.C., Kale, L., Buch, R., Acun, B.: NAMD: scalable molecular dynamics based on the charm++ parallel runtime system. In: Exascale Scientific Applications, pp. 119–144. Chapman and Hall/CRC (2017)
63. Phillips, J.C., Sun, Y., Jain, N., Bohm, E.J., Kalé, L.V.: Mapping to irregular torus topologies and other techniques for petascale biomolecular simulation. In: Proceedings of the International Conference for High Performance Computing, Networking, Storage and Analysis, pp. 81–91. IEEE Press (2014)
64. Pino, S., Pollock, L., Chandrasekaran, S.: Exploring translation of OpenMP to OpenACC 2.5: lessons learned. In: 2017 IEEE International Parallel and Distributed Processing Symposium Workshops (IPDPSW), pp. 673–682. IEEE (2017)
65. Plimpton, S.: Fast parallel algorithms for short-range molecular dynamics. J. Comput. Phys. 117(1), 1–19 (1995)
66. Plimpton, S.J.: The LAMMPS molecular dynamics engine (2017). https://www.osti.gov/servlets/purl/1458156
67. Salomon-Ferrer, R., Götz, A.W., Poole, D., Le Grand, S., Walker, R.C.: Routine microsecond molecular dynamics simulations with AMBER on GPUs. 2. Explicit solvent particle mesh Ewald. J. Chem. Theory Comput. 9(9), 3878–3888 (2013)
68. Schach, S.R.: Object-oriented and Classical Software Engineering, pp. 215–255. McGraw-Hill, New York (2002)
69. Schlick, T.: Molecular Modeling and Simulation: An Interdisciplinary Guide, vol. 21. Springer, New York (2010). https://doi.org/10.1007/978-1-4419-6351-2
70. Sedova, A., Banavali, N.K.: Geometric patterns for neighboring bases near the stacked state in nucleic acid strands. Biochemistry 56(10), 1426–1443 (2017)

71. Shi, T., Belkin, M., Yu, B., et al.: Data spectroscopy: eigenspaces of convolution operators and clustering. Ann. Stat. **37**(6B), 3960–3984 (2009)
72. Solomonik, E., Kale, L.V.: Highly scalable parallel sorting. In: 2010 IEEE International Symposium on Parallel & Distributed Processing (IPDPS), pp. 1–12. IEEE (2010)
73. Stone, J.E., Hynninen, A.-P., Phillips, J.C., Schulten, K.: Early experiences porting the NAMD and VMD molecular simulation and analysis software to GPU-accelerated OpenPOWER platforms. In: Taufer, M., Mohr, B., Kunkel, J.M. (eds.) ISC High Performance 2016. LNCS, vol. 9945, pp. 188–206. Springer, Cham (2016). https://doi.org/10.1007/978-3-319-46079-6_14
74. Sultana, N., Calvert, A., Overbey, J.L., Arnold, G.: From OpenACC to OpenMP 4: toward automatic translation. In: Proceedings of the XSEDE16 Conference on Diversity, Big Data, and Science at Scale, p. 44. ACM (2016)
75. Sun, Y., et al.: Evaluating performance tradeoffs on the Radeon open compute platform. In: 2018 IEEE International Symposium on Performance Analysis of Systems and Software (ISPASS), pp. 209–218. IEEE (2018)
76. Tedre, M., Denning, P.J.: Shifting identities in computing: from a useful tool to a new method and theory of science. Informatics in the Future, pp. 1–16. Springer, Cham (2017). https://doi.org/10.1007/978-3-319-55735-9_1
77. Wienke, S., Springer, P., Terboven, C., an Mey, D.: OpenACC—first experiences with real-world applications. In: Kaklamanis, C., Papatheodorou, T., Spirakis, P.G. (eds.) Euro-Par 2012. LNCS, vol. 7484, pp. 859–870. Springer, Heidelberg (2012). https://doi.org/10.1007/978-3-642-32820-6_85
78. Wienke, S., Terboven, C., Beyer, J.C., Müller, M.S.: A pattern-based comparison of OpenACC and OpenMP for accelerator computing. In: Silva, F., Dutra, I., Santos Costa, V. (eds.) Euro-Par 2014. LNCS, vol. 8632, pp. 812–823. Springer, Cham (2014). https://doi.org/10.1007/978-3-319-09873-9_68

Using OpenMP

OpenMP Code Offloading: Splitting GPU Kernels, Pipelining Communication and Computation, and Selecting Better Grid Geometries

Artem Chikin$^{(\boxtimes)}$, Tyler Gobran, and José Nelson Amaral

University of Alberta, Edmonton, AB, Canada
{artem,gobran,jamaral}@ualberta.ca

Abstract. This paper presents three ideas that focus on improving the execution of high-level parallel code in GPUs. The first addresses programs that include multiple parallel blocks within a single region of GPU code. A proposed compiler transformation can split such regions into multiple, leading to the launching of multiple kernels, one for each parallel region. Advantages include the opportunity to tailor grid geometry of each kernel to the parallel region that it executes and the elimination of the overheads imposed by a code-generation scheme meant to handle multiple nested parallel regions. Second, is a code transformation that sets up a pipeline of kernel execution and asynchronous data transfer. This transformation enables the overlap of communication and computation. Intricate technical details that are required for this transformation are described. The third idea is that the selection of a grid geometry for the execution of a parallel region must balance the GPU occupancy with the potential saturation of the memory throughput in the GPU. Adding this additional parameter to the geometry selection heuristic can often yield better performance at lower occupancy levels.

1 Introduction

Open Multi-Processing (OpenMP) is a widely used parallel programming model that enables offloading of computation to accelerator devices such as GPUs [3]. A natural way for an experienced OpenMP CPU programmer to write OpenMP GPU code is to offload to an accelerator sections of code that contain various parallelism-specifying constructs, that are often adjacent. However, this programming style generally leads to unnecessary overheads that are not apparent to programmers unfamiliar with GPU programming and mapping of high-level OpenMP code to GPUs. Experienced GPU Programmers will instead create a common device data environment and operate on data by invoking separate kernels for each required parallel operation. This technique results in more efficient code and often reduces the overall amount of host-device data transfer, as our work will demonstrate. The main goal of this investigation is to deliver better

© Springer Nature Switzerland AG 2019
S. Chandrasekaran et al. (Eds.): WACCPD 2018 Workshop, LNCS 11381, pp. 51–74, 2019.
https://doi.org/10.1007/978-3-030-12274-4_3

performance for the code written by experienced OpenMP programmers that
are not necessarily GPU programming experts.

When an OpenMP `target` region contains a combination of parallel and
serial work to be executed in a GPU, the compiler must map these computations to the GPU's native Single Instruction, Multiple Thread (SIMT) programming model. One approach is through a technique called warp[1] specialization [2].
When specializing warps, the compiler designates one warp as the master warp
and all others as a pool of worker warps. In the Clang-YKT compiler OpenMP
4 implementation, the master warp is responsible both for executing serial code
and for organization and synchronization of parallel sections [6,7]. The synchronization between parallel and serial work is implemented through named warp
barriers and an emulated stack in GPU global memory for the worker warps to
access the master threads state.

Figure 1 is an example of OpenMP 4 code. The pragma in line 1 establishes
that the following region of code will run on the default target accelerator—
assumed to be a GPU in this work, and ensures that the data specified in `map`
clauses is transferred to and from the GPU, respective to the (`to`, `from`) spec-
ifiers. The pragmas in lines 2 and 6 establish the associated work as parallel
within the enclosing target region. There is an implicit synchronization point at
the end of each parallel region.

```
1  #pragma omp target teams map(to: B[:S]) map(tofrom: A[:S], C[:S]) {
2    #pragma omp distribute parallel for
3    for () {
4    ... // Parallel work involving A and B
5    }
6    #pragma omp distribute parallel for
7    for () {
8    ... //Parallel work involving B and C
9    }
10 }
```

Fig. 1. Example OpenMP GPU code with multiple parallel loops in a target region.

Warp specialization introduces substantial overhead because the master and
worker warps must synchronize execution when parallel region execution starts
and finishes. Even when there is no sequential code between parallel regions,
synchronization is required between the completion of one parallel region and
the start of another.

The Clang-YKT compiler performs a transformation called *elision* that
removes the warp specialization code, the master-thread stack emulation and
the synchronization code, thus eliminating unnecessary overhead [7]. To be candidate for elision, a target region must contain only one parallel loop and this loop

---

[1] CUDA terminology is used in this paper.

must not contain calls to the OpenMP runtime. A research question posed by our work is: what would be the performance effect of transforming an OpenMP 4 `target` region that contains multiple parallel regions, with or without serial code, into multiple target regions, each with a single parallel region. The goal is to enable the compiler to perform the elision transformation. Special care must be taken to avoid increasing the amount of data transfer between the host and device memory.

This paper explores two additional transformation opportunities, both applicable to any OpenMP code where parallel loops are isolated into their own target regions. The first is the overlapping of data transfer and GPU kernel execution for multiple adjacent target regions. The target regions are wrapped in a common device data environment and through memory-use analysis, a compiler can determine which data is and is not needed until or after a certain point. The second opportunity is to overlap computation with data-transfer by pipelining the loop within a single-loop parallel region in a fashion similar to iterative modulo scheduling [16]. The loop iteration space can be divided into multiple tiles, each resulting in a separate kernel launch, execution of which happens asynchronously with the data transfer for the next tile.

Finally, this target region format allows for better selection of grid geometry tailored to the contained parallel loop. Grid geometry is the number of Cooperative Thread Arrays (CTAs), also known as thread blocks, and the number of threads per CTA that the GPU uses. Grid geometry strongly affects the overall occupancy of the GPU. Tailoring this selection to a specific parallel region can have a significant effect on the performance of that region. However, a single grid geometry must be selected for an entire target region. Therefore, multiple parallel regions in the same target region cannot have individually specialized geometry for each parallel region.

In the remainder of this paper, Sect. 2 describes how kernel splitting enables the elision of runtime calls and barrier synchronization. Section 3 presents a sample code to demonstrate how kernel splitting is performed. Section 4 describes the implementation of asynchronous memory transfers and presents a study of their performance implications. Section 5 explains how these transfers can be used to establish a pipeline between computation and data transfers. Section 6 shows that custom grid geometry must take into consideration the potential saturation of memory bandwidth in the GPU. Section 7 presents the performance study that can be used to predict the potential benefits of the proposed transformations. Section 8 discusses other approaches to use asynchronous transfers and to adjust GPU occupancy to improve performance.

2   Background on Warp Specialization and Elision

GPUs' reliance on a SIMT execution model has a multitude of implications on how compilers generate GPU code from OpenMP. Where possible, parallel constructs must be mapped to a data-parallel structure in order to achieve good performance and efficiently utilize the hardware. However, full breadth of the

OpenMP specification must be supported by a compliant compiler implementation. Thus, the GPU code generator must be able to handle a multitude of constructs that contain both serial and parallel code that may be nested or adjacent within a `target` region.

The compiler used in this work employs a cooperative threading model that utilizes the technique of warp specialization to generate data-parallel GPU code from parallel OpenMP regions [7]. Parallel work is performed by a collection of worker warps and coordinated by a single master warp (selected to be the last warp in a CTA). The coordination between warps is done through the use of a CTA-level synchronization primitive that allows for named barriers that apply to a compiler-specified number of warps to participate in the barrier (`bar.sync $0 $1`). When the master encounters a parallel region, it activates the required number of worker warps and suspends its own execution.

While necessary to support the full breadth of possible OpenMP constructs that can occur in target regions, as well as serial code sections and sibling parallel regions, warp specialization code-generation scheme incurs a significant amount of runtime overhead that can be avoided in select special cases. Not all kernels require the full machinery of the cooperative code-generation scheme. For target regions that are comprised solely of a single parallel loop with no nested OpenMP constructs, and no serial code, the compiler optimizes the generated code by eliding the warp specialization and runtime-managed sections of the code. This optimization results in dramatically simpler generated data-parallel code that eliminates the mentioned overheads.

Elision of the cooperative code-generation scheme and its incurred synchronization points is enabled by target region splitting. Jacob et al. describe how this elision is handled automatically by the Clang-YKT compiler, and present a performance study of elision [7]. Code that is transformed with the splitting method shown in Fig. 2 creates separate target regions that are likely to satisfy all of the above conditions for elision.

3   Fission of Multiple-Parallel-Region Target Regions

When a target region is separated into two target regions, as shown in Fig. 2, each target region is then executed as a separate kernel on the GPU and therefore data transferred for the first region is no longer present for the second region to utilize as is the case when both exist in a single-target region. Figure 2 shows how the single-target region spanning lines 1-10 in Fig. 1 can be split into two separate target regions, one spanning lines 2-5 and the other lines 6-9. The parallel region directives (lines 2 and 6 of Fig. 1) are combined with the target directives (lines 2 and 6 of Fig. 2), transforming each parallel region into a stand-alone target construct. To avoid extra data transfers, the newly formed target regions are enclosed in a common device data environment containing all the implicit and explicit mappings of data from the original single-target region. Only the data items specified in the data environment persist in GPU global memory across multiple target regions. The motivation for this transformation to be performed by a compiler is further reinforced by the design of the **kernels** OpenACC construct [1]. **kernels** construct definition states: "The compiler will split the code in the kernels region into a sequence of accelerator kernels", as deemed appropriate by the implementation. This design makes a strong argument for implementing the proposed transformation at the OpenMP level to further the efforts towards performance portability.

```
1   #pragma omp target data map(to: B[:S]) map(tofrom: A[:S], C[:S]) {
2     #pragma omp target teams distribute parallel for
3     for () {
4       ... // Parallel work involving A and B
5     }
6     #pragma omp target teams distribute parallel for
7     for () {
8       ... //Parallel work involving B and C
9     }
10  }
```

Fig. 2. Example OpenMP code following kernel splitting.

Furthermore, with a common device data environment, it is possible to overlap memory transfers with computation by analyzing when each data element is needed or produced. In our hand-implemented prototype for the transformation the OpenMP **target update** directive is used for these transfers, with the additional **nowait** clause added to allow for asynchronous memory transfers.

Safety measures must be taken when performing target fission, mainly to handle the presence of serial sections within the original single-target region. One concern to address is the possibility of variables being declared for the scope of the original single-target region. These variables reside in GPU memory and exist for the duration of the target region that is their scope, as a result the compiler must ensure that splitting does not interfere with any usages of them. One approach, if possible, is to move the variable declaration onto the CPU and map it to the common device data environment with an **alloc** map clause. Additional care must be taken to then mark such variables as **teams private**, to replicate the semantics of original code. Another approach is to limit the fission transformation such that all code from the declaration of the variable to its final usage resides within a single target region, though this can prevent elision.

A mitigating factor for this concern is that any such interfering declaration within the original single-target region scope must reside in a serial region at the target region scope. Variables declared inside parallel regions are assumed to be thread-local and expire when the parallel code block goes out of scope.

Another safety concern is that of serial code operating on data objects that are modified by previous parallel regions or are utilized by later parallel regions. The compiler must ensure that an updated variable is used by both the serial code and any later parallel regions on the GPU as would be the case with a single-target region wherein all code operates on the same GPU memory. One solution is to place serial code segments on the GPU in their own target regions. A drawback is paying the cost of additional kernel launch to execute serial code. An alternative approach is to execute the serial code on the CPU, with compiler analysis ensuring that any data object used in parallel regions are transferred to and from the device as needed for correctness. These transfers can become costly if they occur frequently, but in some cases run time can be improved significantly by executing serial code on the CPU.

Therefore the kernel splitting method should be applied with caution when the original single-target region has serial code or target region scoped local variables. Such scenarios did not appear in any of the benchmarks tested and likely do not represent a large portion of OpenMP code that can benefit from splitting.

4   Overlapping Data Transfer and Split Kernel Execution

Overlapping data transfer with computation can be an effective strategy to increase performance. Opportunities to benefit from asynchronous data transfers may arise from the splitting of a multi-parallel-region target into multiple single-parallel region targets. To enable the pipelining of data transfers and computation, the compiler must determine the first point of use of data and also when the computation of results is completed and the data is no longer used in the target. After such analysis, a schedule can be created for the pipelining with the overlapping effectively hiding the memory transfer time.

Figures 3 and 4 illustrate how this pipelining, enabled by asynchronous memory transfers, can reduce the overall execution time. In this example, if the runtime of the two kernels are long enough, this transformation results in the costs of the asynchronous memory transfers being entirely hidden.

Fig. 3. Two kernel GPU code structure before asynchronous memory transfer.

Execution of asynchronous memory transfers and their synchronization with kernel execution can be specified manually by a programmer, using two OpenMP 4.5 clauses: `depend` and `nowait`. An OpenMP command with a `depend` clause with an `out` attribute must finish before any command with a `depend` clause with an `in` attribute with the same value. The `nowait` clause states that the specified OpenMP task can be run asynchronously with other tasks, thus allowing the update memory transfer to occur while a target region is executing. The combination of these clauses allows for the construction of GPU code that has asynchronous memory transfers to and from the GPU while also maintaining correct computation through clearly established task dependence relations by which these asynchronous transfers must finish.

Figure 5 is an example of split target region code with asynchronous memory transfers within a common device data environment. In this example the data element C is not needed until the target region at line 9, thus its mapping in the **target data** region in line 2 is only to return to the host after all work finishes. The transfer to the GPU for C instead begins on line 3 where it is declared asynchronous by the **nowait** clause. With the pair of **depend** clauses in lines 3 and 9 ensuring the transfer must be completed before any computation on the target region in line 9 can begin. Furthermore the array A can be transferred back to the host memory asynchronously as it is not used in the second target region. Thus the memory transfer of A back to the host is moved to line 8, after the first target region computation and it is declared to be asynchronous.

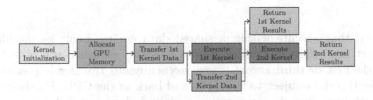

Fig. 4. Two kernel GPU code structure with asynchronous memory transfer.

As per vendor specification, asynchronous memory transfers require that the transferred data be page-locked i.e. *pinned* on the host. A pinned page cannot be swapped out to disk and enables DMA transfers via the memory controller, bypassing the CPU. To enable asynchronous transfers, the pinning must be done through the CUDA API to allocate/free pinned memory or to pin pre-allocated heap memory. The invocation of these API functions and the actual pinning of the memory introduce additional overheads but also leads to faster memory transfers. Memory capacity constraints of the target device are not affected by the transformed kernel. The amount of data required to be present on the device at a given time is reduced in the best case, and is left unaffected in the worst.

We use the **cudaHostRegister** API to pin user-allocated memory in our experiments. The main trade-off to consider when implementing kernel asynchronous data transfers is to offset the overhead of pinning memory through faster transfers enabled by pinned memory and overlapping transfer with computation. Pinning memory also has the effect of reducing the overall memory available on the host for other processes, which can possibly stifle host computation. An important factor to consider when pinning memory is the operating system's default page size. We have found that pinning the same amount of memory was up to 10× faster on a POWER8 host with 64 KB pages than on a x86 Haswell host with 4 KB pages.

A synthetic experiment to illustrate the balancing of the costs and benefits of asynchronous memory transfer was designed with three simple GPU kernels

```
1  int a;
2  #pragma omp targe data map(to: A[:S], B[:S]) map(from: C[:S]) {
3    #pragma omp target update to(C[:S]) depend(out: a) nowait
4    #pragma omp target teams distribute parallel for
5    for () {
6      ... // Parallel work involving A and B
7    }
8    #pragma omp target update from(A[:S]) nowait
9    #pragma omp target teams distribute parallel for depend(in: a)
10   for () {
11     ... //Parallel work involving B and C
12   }
13 }
```

Fig. 5. The split OpenMP GPU code with asynchronous memory transfers.

(k_1, k_2, k_3) that execute within a shared data environment; k_2 modifies one data object from the CPU whose results must be returned, the object is not used by the first or third kernel. Thus, asynchronous transfer is possible both to transfer this data object to the GPU and back to the CPU. Furthermore, k_1 and k_3 both have enough computation to fully hide the asynchronous memory transfers. The experiment's results with a varying size of the object modified by k_2 are shown in Fig. 6. The baseline version uses unpinned memory and synchronous transfers. Four versions using pinned memory were constructed for comparison: (1) sync transfers; (2) async to/sync from; (3) sync to/async from; (4) async to/async from. The run time measured includes the time needed to allocate and free memory. The graph outlines the speedup ratio in total execution time for each of the four pinned memory versions compared to the baseline version. The horizontal axis shows both the size of the object transferred and the baseline run time measured in seconds. The results show that as the size of the transferred object increases, the additional cost of pinning memory becomes less relevant. For larger objects, even though simply pinning the memory pages yields performance gains, asynchronous memory transfers produce additional benefits.

5   Pipelining Data Transfer and Parallel Loop Execution

A more ambitious code transformation that utilizes the faster transfer to/from pinned memory and asynchronous communication and computation consists of breaking a singular parallel loop into multiple loops. Known as *tiling* in compiler literature, this transformation produces multiple sub-loops (tiles) which are then placed in separate target regions. After this transformation the data transfer required for the original loop may be split into several asynchronous data transfers for data elements required by the respective tiles. Ideally, each tile should use different, contiguous, large chunks of data. The goal is to overlap

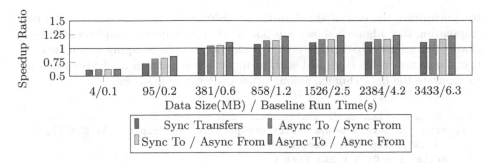

Fig. 6. Speedup of the four versions pinning memory over the baseline version.

the transfer with computation. In the evaluation prototype OpenMP `depend` clauses are used to ensure that each data transfer is finished before the corresponding tile executes. Transmission of tile results back to the host can also be added to this pipeline. Pipelining can greatly improve the run-time performance of programs with large data transfers, when the execution time of the split loop is long enough to compensate for the overhead of setting up data transfers and pinning memory.

Figure 7 illustrates how the execution of a parallel region can be pipelined to overlap memory transfers with computation. The single parallel-loop GPU kernel is split into four tiles which allows the memory transfers required for the latter three tiles to be hidden underneath the previous tiles' execution with asynchronous transfers. Furthermore if the execution of the tiles are long enough to cover the runtime of the memory transfers then the total cost of the transfers may be as low as 1/4 of the original cost.

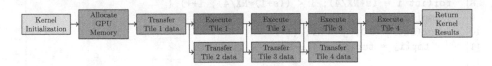

Fig. 7. A GPU parallel regions structure after being broken up into 4 tiles.

The Polybench benchmark `ATAX` is a good candidate to benefit from this transformation. The original benchmark's first parallel region, shown in Fig. 8, has the majority of its runtime dependent on the memory transfer of the data object A to the GPU in line 1. Figure 9 shows the code after the loop is divided into four tiles and the transfer of A split into four OpenMP `target update` calls. The first call in line 2 is not asynchronous as it must be done before the first tile execution starts. The remaining three transfers in line 6 are asynchronous and start before the preceding tile execution to overlap communication and computation. The `depend` clauses in the asynchronous transfers are needed to synchronize the end of the data transmission with the execution of the corresponding tile. Figure 9 shows a proof-of-concept manually implemented code change. A sufficiently-capable compiler should be able to apply a similar code transformation when equipped with memory access-pattern analysis to be able to separate tile data chunks, among other code safety analyses.

```
1  #pragma omp target teams distribute parallel for map(to: A[:NX*NY], x
       [ :NY]) map(from: tmp[:NX]) {
2    for(int i = 0; i < NX; i++) {
3      tmp[i] = 0;
4      for(int j = 0; j < NY; j++)
5        tmp[i] = tmp[i] + A[i*NY+j] * x[j];
6    }
7  }
```

Fig. 8. First parallel region in `ATAX` before pipelining.

```
1  int S[4];
2  #pragma omp target update to(A[0:(NX/4)*NY])
3  for(int s = 0; s < 4; s++)
4  {
5    if (s < 3)
6      #pragma omp target update to(A[((s+1)*NX/4)*NY:((s+2)*NX/4)*NY])
           depend(out: S[s+1]) nowait
7    #pragma omp target teams distribute parallel for depend(in: S[s])
8    for(int i = (s*NX/4); i < ((s+1)*NX/4); i++) {
9      tmp[i] = 0;
10     for(int j = 0; j < NY; j++)
11       tmp[i] = tmp[i] + A[i*NY+j] * x[j];
12   }
13 }
```

Fig. 9. `ATAX` region after being broken up into four tiles for pipelining.

6   Custom Grid Geometry

A grid geometry defines the number of CTAs and the number of threads per CTA assigned to execute a GPU kernel. A typical GPU has a number of Streaming Multiprocessor (SM) cores that can each issue instructions for two groups of 32 threads (warps) in each cycle. An SM can maintain the state of thousands of threads in-flight, and thus can context switch execution from a warp waiting on data accesses to other warps in order to hide memory-access latency.

Each SM has a fixed-size register file, giving each CTA a register budget. At any given time the number of CTAs that can be scheduled is limited by the size of the register file. Similarly, each SM has a fixed amount of shared memory which is shared by all CTAs running on the SM. Thus, the number of CTAs simultaneously executing on an SM is also constrained by the individual CTA's shared memory use. Additional CTAs that cannot be scheduled due to these and other hardware resource limitations are queued for later execution. GPU occupancy is the percentage of available GPU threads that are used by a given kernel.

Some parallel regions with relatively low parallelism perform better when not using all available threads. A compiler can analyze parallel loops in a target region to select the most performant grid geometry. However, a single grid geometry has to be selected for an entire target region leading to a compromise that performs relatively well for all the loop nests in the region. Grid geometry specialized to each individual parallel loop, made possible by target region fission, can lead to significant performance improvements.

Lloyd et al. propose a compiler heuristic, based on static analysis and runtime loop tripcount data, for the selection of a grid geometry calculated by the amount of parallelism in each loop nest [13]. The heuristic takes into account the usage of registers and shared memory for each thread and CTA as it seeks to maximize the GPU occupancy. However, maximizing occupancy can often lead to far worse performance because it leads to saturation of other hardware resource, such as the memory subsystem in heavily memory-bound codes. An example of this effect occurs in the SYRK benchmark shown in Fig. 10. At a tripcount of 4000 the best performance is achieved around 25% occupancy which is close to the Clang-YKT default of roughly 28.6% (128 CTAs on this GPU). For this case the heuristic proposed by Lloyd makes a poor choice of geometry because in seeking to maximize occupancy it does not consider memory-bandwidth saturation. Maximum occupancy produces a Unified Cache throughput of 19.742 GB/s compared to a throughput of 183.001 GB/s at the optimal occupancy of 25%; moreover, the observed Global Load Throughput of 751.8 GB/s at optimal occupancy versus 81.5 GB/s at maximal, and the respective Global Store Throughput is 91.5 and 9.9 GB/s. These metrics support the intuition that memory bus saturation can severely limit performance at high occupancy.

This exception to the grid geometry formula led to the formulation of an improved grid-geometry selection strategy for the cases where the optimal occupancy is lower than the maximum. These cases fall into the broad category of parallel regions with a high amount of parallelism exposed by the program (high parallel-loop tripcounts) and result from memory-bandwidth saturation due to a large number of memory requests. The results of this performance study allows for the classification of these cases of massively parallel memory-bound kernels into two subcategories:

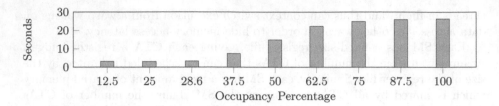

Fig. 10. Runtime results by occupancy of SYRK at tripcount 4000.

Uncoalesced Kernels are highly memory-bound due to uncoalesced memory accesses in large tripcount parallel loops. Uncoalesced memory accesses being loads and stores to global memory where data locations accessed by adjacent threads in a warp are not grouped together closely enough, hence the warp must perform several memory accesses to satisfy all the threads in a warp. This subcategory includes the benchmarks SYRK with tripcount of 1000 or higher and COVAR with tripcounts of 12000 or higher. SYRK falls into this subcategory due to the two high tripcount outer loops of its longest running parallel region being collapsed for high parallelism and an innermost loop containing an uncoalesced memory access which is performed sequentially by each thread. COVAR has a similar structure except without a collapse of the two outer loops and two uncoalesced memory accesses instead of one inside the inner loop. A close examination of the execution of the SYRK benchmark in the Nvidia Visual Profiler, reveals that the best performance is observed when the ratio between attempted memory transaction count and the memory throughput is the lowest—when the most data is transferred with the fewest requests. The grid geometry affects this ratio because more warps generate more requests when memory accesses are not coalesced.

The SYRK performance study shown in Fig. 10 indicates that there is an opportunity to improve the grid-geometry selection by taking into consideration memory-bandwidth saturation. In a supplementary performance study we altered the ratio of requests/memory throughput in SYRK by adding and removing dummy uncoalesced memory accesses. This study yielded a pattern of optimal occupancy halving roughly when the number of uncoalesced memory accesses double. This insight can be used to predict the optimal occupancy for a parallel region. To analyze this pattern further a synthetic experiment was designed in which a more generalized program similar to SYRK was created consisting of a simple summation of the rows of k different $N \times N$ matrices to produce a single matrix. The summation statement is performed within a triple-nested loop with each tripcount being 5000 and the summation involves exclusively uncoalesced memory accesses (row-major matrix accesses). The experiment was then performed with different numbers of uncoalesced memory accesses to find the optimal occupancy for each. The results of the experiment in Table 1 show the similar optimal occupancy pattern that was found in the study of SYRK, indicating a general pattern. This study and experiment indicates that the heuristic for grid-geometry selection introduced by Lloyd et al. should be augmented to account for memory-request saturation [13].

Table 1. Optimal occupancy for a massively parallel memory-bound kernel at varying numbers of uncoalesced memory accesses with tripcount 5000.

Number of accesses	1	2	3	4	5	6	7	8	9	10
Optimal occupancy	25%	12.5%	6.3%	6.3%	6.3%	6.3%	6.3%	4.0%	4.0%	3.1%

Coalesced Kernels have high memory utilization because of parallel loops with very large tripcounts and several memory accesses. Coalesced memory accesses are the opposite of uncoalesced and require only one access to bring over all data required by a warp of threads. This category includes the benchmarks FDTD-2D and LUD at high tripcounts. Lower occupancy results in better performance but the effect is less significant as shown in the results for the experiment study of FDTD-2D in Fig. 11. This category should also be taken into consideration in an augmented version of the grid-geometry-selection heuristic.

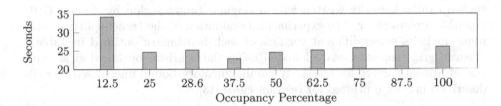

Fig. 11. Runtime results by occupancy of FDTD-2D at tripcount 15000.

7   Estimating Potential Benefits of Transformations

The goal of this experimental evaluation is to estimate the potential performance benefits of the proposed transformations to inform a design-team's decision to include them in a compiler. The results in this section are based on manually-implemented modifications to programs in the Polybench and Rodinia benchmark suites [4, 5]. Both suites have an initial OpenMP 4.0 implementation. Before performing the experiments, we modified some programs in both suites to fully utilize the GPU parallelism hierarchy with **teams** and **distribute** constructs. This experimental study uses benchmarks that contain parallel regions where the three transformations described in the paper can be applied. SPEC ACCEL benchmarks, while available to us for experimentation, contain few to none such cases. Therefore, they do not make a good case for the transformation described in this work due to their already-extensive usage of `target data` data-sharing environments.

All performance results reported are the average of ten runs of the program under the same conditions. Measurement variances were monitored and stayed below 1% of the average and are not reported. Two exceptions are in the execution of `SYRK` and `COVAR` that saw up to 5% variance from the average because of the effects of memory saturation. Correctness of every transformation was verified using the benchmarks' output verification mechanisms.

This experimental study uses an x86 host equipped with an Intel i7-4770 processor, 32 GiB of RAM and an NVIDIA Titan X Pascal GPU with 28 SMs and 12 GiB of on-board memory that is attached via the PCIe bus. The clock rate is locked at 80% of the nominal clock rate for the GPU to prevent variance in performance due to frequency scaling[2]. Additional experiments are performed using an IBM POWER8 (8335-GTB) host with an Nvidia P100 GPU with 60 SMs that is attached via NVLINK.

7.1   Combining Kernel Splitting with Elision Improves Performance

The effect of the transformation on performance is studied on `2MM`, `3MM`, `FDTD-2D`, `SYRK`, `COVAR`, `ATAX`, `MVT` and `BICG` applications from the Polybench benchmark suite and `SRAD` and `LUD` from the Rodinia benchmark suite. All benchmarks chosen can be logically written with a singular target region by a naive GPU OpenMP programmer. The experimental evaluation of the kernel-splitting technique includes seven different versions of each benchmark outlined in Table 2. Custom grid geometry was calculated using the heuristic by Lloyd et al. with the additional pattern for massively parallel memory-bound uncoalesced kernels described in Sect. 6 utilized for relevant cases [13].

Table 2. The experimental evaluation versions for the splitting method.

Version	Kernel splitting	Elision	Custom grid geometry
Baseline			
K	✓		
KE	✓	✓	
KEG	✓	✓	✓

Figure 12 displays the speedup over the baseline for each benchmark and each version shown in Table 2. Asynchronous transfer is not applicable (N/A) to the `SRAD`, `FDTD-2D` and `LUD` benchmarks as they all lack memory transfers that could be performed asynchronously. In the baseline, serial code is executed between

---

[2] Dynamic frequency scaling makes achieving consitent, reproducible results very challenging due to high variance and increased effects of device warm-up.

any two parallel regions and the state of the master thread is propagated to all worker threads. Kernel splitting removes the serial code and workers' update. LUD has few worker threads because of its low level of parallelism, thus there is little benefit to the elimination of worker updating and the cost of launching a second kernel makes LUD slower after splitting (version K). LUD's target region is executed within a loop, which amplifies the cost of the extra kernel launch. In contrast, FDTD-2D and SRAD have far higher levels of parallelism which leads to more expensive workers' state update. Thus they benefit the most from kernel splitting.

Benchmark	Base Time	K	KE	KEG
2MM	36.6s	1.00	0.85	1.22
3MM	54.8s	1.00	0.85	1.22
FDTD-2D	11.8s	1.03	1.23	1.37
SYRK	40.9s	1.00	0.92	1.04
COVAR	54.9s	1.00	1.04	1.04
ATAX	0.16s	1.01	1.03	1.03
MVT	0.16s	1.01	1.00	1.02
BICG	0.16s	1.00	1.01	1.01
SRAD	8.90s	1.04	1.45	1.48
LUD	38.1s	0.91	1.57	1.57

Fig. 12. The speedup ratio over the baseline for each experiment evaluation of the applicable Polybench and Rodinia benchmarks run at a tripcount set to 9600. SRAD executes on a 512by512 image with the encompassing iteration loop performed 9600 times. LUD operates on a 9600by9600 matrix.

Benefits from adding elision to splitting (version KE) vary, with 2MM, 3MM and SYRK performing poorly because the runtime's default strategy selects an inefficient grid geometry. The removal of the warp specialization and sequential code overhead makes the memory bus saturation issue more relevant leading to the lower performance. In SYRK the main issue is that the default occupancy is too high. In 2MM and 3MM the number of threads is too low to exploit all available parallelism. FDTD-2D, SRAD, and LUD benefit greatly from elision because they contain a large number of kernel calls, accumulating the reduction in overhead of the elided kernels over time. Moreover, the amount of parallelism and the compute-bound nature of the kernels in these benchmarks suit the compiler's default grid geometry selection strategy.

Asynchronous memory transfer (version KA) by itself produces either negligible benefits or performance degradation. The degradation for ATAX, MVT and BICG results from the small size of data objects making the cost of pinning the data for transfer far greater then any hidden transfer cost and the short length of the benchmarks emphasizes this.

In general, significant performance improvements are achieved by the kernel-splitting technique combined with elision for the given benchmarks. Furthermore, any poor performance can be mitigated by additional procedures such as tuning grid geometry that are only available once the splitting technique is applied.

7.2 Elision Amplifies Benefits of Custom Grid Geometry

SYRK and COVAR are the benchmarks most affected by the grid-geometry selection. Both are highly memory-bound because they contain frequently executed uncoalesced memory accesses (SYRK has one, and COVAR has two) and as a result they both have lower than maximum optimal occupancies that produce large performance improvements. COVAR only has a lower than maximum optimal occupancy at higher tripcounts as it lacks the high parallelism of SYRK. These benchmarks' optimal occupancies decrease as the number of memory accesses rise with higher tripcounts, the optimal percentages following the optimal-occupancy trend outlined in Table 1.

Further experimental evaluation of SYRK and COVAR at multiple tripcounts for both a base unsplit version and a KEG version illustrates the effects of varying the grid geometry. The optimal occupancy, determined by the grid geometry, changes with the amount of parallelism for both benchmarks. For SYRK the optimal occupancy is 25% at lower tripcounts and 18.75% at higher tripcounts, while for COVAR the optimal is the default heuristic presented by Lloyd et al. that has the occupancy slowly grow towards the maximum for lower tripcounts when parallelism is low, with higher tripcounts having an optimal occupancy of 12.5% [13]. To illustrate this shift of optimal occupancy the experimental results shown in Fig. 13 present the speedups of the two benchmarks' KEG version over the baseline for both of their optimal occupancies. The large improvement for SYRK at tripcount 3000 matches a similar effect in other programs with collapsed parallel loops that is caused by a sufficiently high parallelism. This performance is due to a combination of a GPU code that was simplified by elision and low impact of memory bus saturation because of still relatively low parallelism.

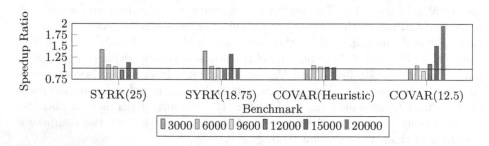

Fig. 13. Speedup over the baseline for the KEG version of the two benchmarks at their two improved occupancies with varying tripcounts. Heuristic refers to that by Lloyd et al. [13]

2MM, 3MM and FDTD-2D present slight performance degradation when only custom grid geometry is applied (version KG) as with all three benchmarks the custom grid geometry is set to achieve full occupancy of the GPU SM's. With elision this is optimal but without elision additional warps are added on top of the full occupancy for the master warps in each CTA. As a result the executed kernels request more warps then can be active on the GPU concurrently, thus additional scheduling of the warps is performed by the GPU to ensure all warps execute. This scheduling causes overhead that result in worse performance for the three benchmarks compared to when only kernel-splitting is applied. In comparison significant performance improvements for SRAD with version KG come from the high amount of computation compared to memory accesses in the program which take advantage of increased GPU occupancy from the heuristic.

The improvements brought by custom grid geometry (version KG) are amplified when combined with elision (version KEG) because the simplified execution for elided code better utilizes an optimized number of CTAs in terms of memory utilization and computation ability. Thus, the version KEG produces the best performance through this amplification of the benefits of elision and custom grid geometry.

Finally asynchronous transfers do not interact with grid geometry in any meaningful way, as such the KEGA results are only presented for completeness.

7.3   Pipelining Improves Performance for High Trip Counts

The pipelining transformation requires that a parallel region be broken into sub-loops that process separate data chunks of sufficiently large size to justify the pipeline. Thus only the Polybench benchmarks ATAX, GESUMMV and GEMM are suitable for pipelining. Memory transfers to/from the GPU are dominant for the execution time for ATAX and GESUMMV resulting in significant improvements from pipelining. These improvements increase with the number of iterations as the additional computation amortizes the cost of pinning memory pages. Pipelining transfers plays a minor role in GEMM because kernel execution is dominant, instead the restructuring of computation caused by splitting the kernel in four improves performance. Each of the four resulting kernels have a quarter of the parallelism of the original kernel and thus a higher number of loop iterations can be executed before memory bandwidth saturation requires reduction in occupancy. A similar effect occurs for ATAX and GESUMMV but due to the dominant memory transfers the effect on performance is minimal.

For the experimental evaluation of kernel pipelining on the benchmarks ATAX, GESUMMV and GEMM, the baseline is a KE version of the benchmarks with non-pinned memory for all data objects. This baseline is compared to a version that has data transfer pipelined into four tiles with all pipelined data objects pinned. Both versions utilize the default Clang-YKT grid geometry formula. The evaluation is run on two machines: the Intel i7-4770 described above and a POWER8 host with a P100 GPU. The results in Fig. 14 show significant improvements in performance with kernel pipelining for sufficiently large tripcounts. The POWER8 speedup is far larger because it uses 64 KB pages compared to the 4 KB pages in the Intel i7. The larger page size greatly reduces the cost of pinning memory. GEMM sees significant performance improvement because each individual

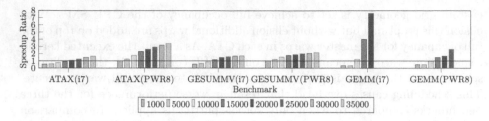

Fig. 14. Speedup over the baseline with the kernel pipelining method on applicable Polybench benchmarks at varying tripcounts. GEMM is missing sizes due to time constraints.

tile processes a smaller chunk of data, thus allowing for higher utilization of the device without hitting the memory subsystem saturation performance barrier. In comparison, the benefits for ATAX and GESUMMV emerge from hiding transfer cost. At lower tripcounts the transformation degrades performance because there is not enough parallelism in the tiles to utilize as many GPU SMs, and the overhead of pinning memory and initializing additional kernels is not overcome.

In a second version of the experiment, on the x86 machine, the optimal occupancy at every tripcount for each kernel is applied to remove the influence of memory saturation. For GESUMMV and GEMM the optimal is 12.5% occupancy for the baseline and the Clang-YKT default formula for the pipelined version. While ATAX has an optimal occupancy of 18.75% for the baseline and the default formula for the pipelined version. Figure 15 shows this experiment's results with significantly better performance for the baseline that lowers the speedup from the pipelined version. However the pipelining still shows benefits due to pipelined memory transfers and later memory saturation at higher tripcounts of the benchmarks.

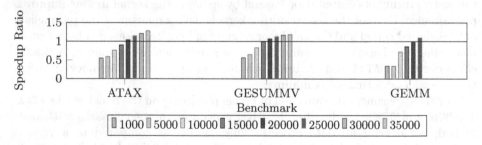

Fig. 15. Speedup over the baseline for the kernel pipelining method on an Intel i7 machine at varying tripcounts with optimal occupancy applied to all kernels.

8   Related Work

Asynchronous transfers are used for BigKernel, by Mokhtari et al., which breaks up a kernel into smaller kernels and pipelines memory transfer in a similar fashion to our kernel pipelining process [14]. BigKernel is a coding framework wherein a memory transfer that would be too large for the available GPU memory is partitioned into segments which are then transferred onto the GPU as needed. The data segments are laid out by BigKernel in host memory by analyzing the GPU kernel and organizing all data items that are used into a prefetch buffer in the order of their access by the GPU threads, creating more coalesced memory accesses in the GPU as memory accessed at the same time is placed beside each other. As with our pipelining method these transfers are performed asynchronously and are overlapped with unrelated kernel computation. However, BigKernel requires a programmer to specify different GPU calls as opposed to the compiler transformation that we propose. Furthermore, BigKernel focuses on very large data and thus its design requires double the original number of threads for a kernel, with half the threads utilized for calculating prefetch addresses. These additional overheads are not present in our method.

A common approach to pipeline GPU execution uses double buffering. Komoda et al. present a OpenCL library that optimize CPU-GPU communication by overlapping computation and memory transfers based on simple program-descriptions written by the programmer [10]. Komoda's work is limited to pipelining memory transfers with existing GPU kernels, and requires programmer specification. Our approach, in contrast, creates multiple kernels out of a single description of a GPU program (a single `target` region) to enable pipelining.

GPU occupancy is the focus of Kayıran et al.'s DYNCTA, a dynamic solution similar to ours that accounts for memory saturation by reducing occupancy [8]. DYNCTA analyzes each GPU SM's utilization and memory latency during execution and adjusts the occupancy within the SM to avoid memory-bandwidth saturation by keeping occupancy lower than the maximum. Changing the defined grid geometry for a kernel is impossible, as a result occupancy adjustment is achieved by assigning additional CTAs to a SM that have already been allocated to the kernel at the start of execution. Once assigned to an SM a CTA cannot be removed, as a result adjustment is performed by prioritizing or deprioritizing CTAs. A prioritized CTA has any available warps executed before a deprioritized CTA's warps, as a result with memory intensive programs wherein all warps stall on memory accesses the deprioritized CTAs will eventually be utilized after all prioritized warps stall. Performance is improved by having the occupancy just below the threshold where memory saturation causes negative effects, ensuring the SM remains utilized while avoiding the punishing effects of memory saturation. Analysis is recorded in two hardware counters within each SM, that record how long each SM has been under utilized and how the often the SM has stalled due to memory access waiting. Sethia et al. describe a similar approach with Equalizer, a heuristic that dynamically adjusts the number of CTAs based on four hardware counters [18]. Lee et al. propose a slightly different strategy with "Lazy CTA Scheduling" (LCS) wherein the workload of an initial prioritized CTA is calculated by a hardware performance counter and that data is used to calculate an improved number of CTAs for each SM [11]. In contrast, our grid geometry proposal is based on a simple hybrid analysis with a low runtime cost and is suitable for simple GPU kernels, which represent the majority of benchmarks we have tested. The benefits of a simple heuristic approach over heavyweight dynamic mechanisms, as outlined by Lloyd et al. allow for a practical deployment in a production system, even if it does sacrifice some optimality [13].

Sethia et al. present the Mascar system, which approaches memory saturation by prioritizing the accesses of a single warp instead of a round robin approach [17]. The single warp starts computation earlier to help hide the latency of other accesses, with the scheduler additionally prioritizing warps with computation over memory-accessing warps when memory saturation is detected. A queue for failed L1 cache access attempts is also added to the GPU hardware, holding the accesses for later execution, it prevents warps from saturating the cache controller with repeated access requests so that other warps can attempt their accesses. Mascar requires hardware design and warp scheduling changes. In contrast, our custom grid geometry based on static analysis is far less intrusive.

Other dynamic approaches include Oh et al.'s APRES, a predictive warp scheduler that prioritizes the scheduling of groups of warps with likely cache hits [15]. Kim et al. suggest an additional P-mode for warps waiting on long memory accesses wherein later instructions that are independent of the long accesses are pre-executed while any dependent operations are skipped [9]. Lee et al.'s CAWA reduces the disparity in execution time between warps by providing the slower running warps with more time to execute and a reserved area of the L1 cache [12]. All these approaches have additional run time costs when compared to a static analysis and compile-time selection of custom grid geometry and re-distribution of work across multiple kernels enabled by pipelining. Furthermore, warp scheduling approaches and custom grid geometries are complimentary and can be combined.

9 Conclusion

This paper puts forward the idea of splitting a singular OpenMP target region of GPU code with multiple parallel regions into multiple target regions each with a singular parallel region. The experimental evaluation using Polybench and Rodinia benchmarks indicates that there can be non-trivial performance gains from implementing this idea in future compilers targeting OpenMP 4.x. Additionally the evaluation indicates that combining kernel splitting with synchronization elision and support for asynchronous memory transfers (with OpenMP 4.5) would lead to even more significant performance.

The study of grid geometry indicates that there is scope to improve existing grid-geometry selection strategy by considering the saturation of the GPU memory bandwidth due to uncoalesced memory accesses or to data-intensive parallel loop nests. This problem was recognized before with both dynamic run-time solutions and hardware changes proposed. However, the solution proposed here based on static analysis and compiler action is simpler, effective, and has lower overhead.

This paper also studies the performance effect of pipelining memory transfers with kernel execution when there is sufficient data. Both kernel splitting and loop tiling can be used to enable pipelining. The results indicate that the performance gains can be significant especially in machines with larger page sizes such as the POWER architecture.

Acknowledgements. This research was supported by the IBM Canada Software Lab Centre for Advanced Studies (CAS) and by the National Science and Engineering Research Council (NSERC) of Canada through their Collaborative Research and Development (CRD) program and through the Undergraduate Student Research Awards (USRA) program.

A   Artifact Description Appendix: OpenMP Target Offloading: Splitting GPU Kernels, Pipelining Communication and Computation, and Selecting Better Grid Geometries

A.1   Abstract

This artifact contains the code for our experimental evaluations of the kernel splitting and kernel pipelining methods with instructions to run the benchmark versions to replicate all experimental results from Sect. 7.

A.2   Description

Check-List

- **Program:** C code, Python3 code
- **Compilation:** Prototype of Clang-YKT compiler used
- **Transformations:** Kernel-Splitting, Kernel-Pipelining
- **Hardware:** Intel i7-4770 with Nvidia Titan X Pascal, IBM POWER8 (8335-GTB) with Nvidia P100 GPU
- **Software:** x86: Ubuntu 18.04 LTS, Cuda V9.1.85; POWER: RHEL Server 7.3, Cuda V9.2.88
- **Experiment workflow:** Install Clang-YKT prototype then run the provided benchmarks with the given script
- **Publicly available?:** Yes

How Software Can Be Obtained. Our prototype of the Clang-YKT compiler is available on Github, with our benchmark versions used for all experiments included.

The original Clang-YKT compiler can be found at: https://github.com/clang-ykt/clang

With the commit hash: `49d8020e03f898ea31212f6c565001e067f67d4f`

Hardware Dependencies. An Intel i7-4770 machine with an Nvidia Titan X Pascal GPU was used for almost all experimentation and for similar results an equivalent machine must be utilized. This is especially true for the experiments on occupancy as our optimal occupancies are tied to the Nvidia Titan X Pascal GPU. An additional IBM POWER8 (8335-GTB) host with an Nvidia P100 GPU was used with kernel-pipelining for experimenting with different page sizes and to replicate those results a similar machine must be utilized.

Software Dependencies. A prototype of the Clang-YKT compiler from Github was utilized for compilation of OpenMP code though any compiler that supports OpenMP 4 can be used to run the kernel-splitting and kernel-pipelining benchmark versions.

Datasets. Experiments for each benchmark require only inputting the given tripcount desired for each, with only SRAD requiring an additional pgm image.

A.3   Installation

Clone the Clang-YKT prototype repository (includes all testing files):
```
$ git clone https://github.com/uasys/openmp-split
```
Then install the compiler with the following commands:
```
$ mkdir -p $build
# 60 stands for GPU compute capability
$ cmake DCMAKE_BUILD_TYPE=RELEASE DCMAKE_INSTALL_PREFIX=$CLANGYKT_DIR
DLLVM_ENABLE_BACKTRACES=ON DLLVM_ENABLE_WERROR=OFF DBUILD_SHARED_LIBS=OFF
DLLVM_ENABLE_RTTI=ON DOPENMP_ENABLE_LIBOMPTARGET=ON DCMAKE_C_FLAGS='-
DOPENMP_NVPTX_COMPUTE_CAPABILITY=60'
DCMAKE_CXX_FLAGS='DOPENMP_NVPTX_COMPUTE_CAPABILITY=60'
DLIBOMPTARGET_NVPTX_COMPUTE_CAPABILITY=60
DCLANG_OPENMP_NVPTX_DEFAULT_ARCH=sm_60
DLIBOMPTARGET_NVPTX_ENABLE_BCLIB=true -G Ninja $LLVM_BASE
$ ninja -j4; ninja install
```
After installation the GPU clock rate must be locked at 80% of the nominal clock rate of the GPU to prevent any variation in performance due to frequency scaling when performing the experiments.

To lock the Nvidia Titan X Pascal input:
```
nvidia-smi -pm 1
nvidia-smi -application-clocks=4513,1240
```

A.4   Experiment Workflow

Experimentation is performed by executing the runTest.py file in the given transformations folder with the chosen benchmark's name and the tripcount to run it at. Benchmarks for kernel-splitting and those for kernel-pipelining are held in separate folders.

A.5   Evaluation and Expected Results

The script above will produce a printout once all runs are complete that contains the average run time of each version with the percentage variance and the speedup ratio relative to the baseline.

A.6   Experiment Customization

Adjusting grid geometry can be done by editing the BLOCKS macro values in the benchmark files with a postfix including G which indicate versions with custom grid geometry.

A.7   Notes

None.

References

1. The OpenACC application programming interface. https://www.openacc.org/sites/default/files/inline-files/OpenACC.2.6.final.pdf
2. Bauer, M., Cook, H., Khailany, B.: CudaDMA: optimizing GPU memory bandwidth via warp specialization. In: High Performance Computing, Networking, Storage and Analysis SC, Seattle, WA, USA, pp. 1–11 (2011)
3. OpenMP Architecture Review Board: OpenMP application programming interface. https://www.openmp.org/wp-content/uploads/openmp-4.5.pdf
4. Che, S., et al.: Rodinia: a benchmark suite for heterogeneous computing. In: IEEE International Symposium on Workload Characterization (IISWC), pp. 44–54 (2009)
5. Chikin, A.: Unibench for OpenMP 4.0. https://github.com/artemcm/Unibench
6. Jacob, A.C., et al.: Clang-YKT source-code repository. https://github.com/clang-ykt
7. Jacob, A.C., et al.: Efficient fork-join on GPUs through warp specialization. In: High Performance Computing HiPC, Jaipur, India, pp. 358–367 (2017)
8. Kayıran, O., Jog, A., Kandemir, M.T., Das, C.R.: Neither more nor less: optimizing thread-level parallelism for GPGPUs. In: Parallel Architectures and Compilation Techniques PACT, Piscataway, NJ, USA, pp. 157–166 (2013)
9. Kim, K., Lee, S., Yoon, M.K., Koo, G., Ro, W.W., Annavaram, M.: Warped-preexecution: a GPU pre-execution approach for improving latency hiding. In: High Performance Computer Architecture HPCA, Barcelona, Spain, pp. 163–175 (2016)

10. Komoda, T., Miwa, S., Nakamura, H.: Communication library to overlap computation and communication for OpenCL application. In: Parallel and Distributed Processing Symposium Workshops IPDPSW, Shanghai, China, pp. 567–573 (2012)
11. Lee, M., et al.: Improving GPGPU resource utilization through alternative thread block scheduling. In: High Performance Computer Architecture HPCA, Orlando, FL, USA, pp. 260–271 (2014)
12. Lee, S.-Y., Arunkumar, A., Wu, C.-J.: CAWA: coordinated warp scheduling and cache prioritization for critical warp acceleration of GPGPU workloads. In: International Symposium on Computer Architecture (ISCA), Portland, Oregon, pp. 515–527. ACM (2015)
13. Lloyd, T., Chikin, A., Amaral, J.N., Tiotto, E.: Automated GPU grid geometry selection for OpenMP kernels. In: Workshop on Applications for Multi-Core Architectures, WAMCA 2018, September 2018. Pre-print Manuscript. https://webdocs. cs.ualberta.ca/~amaral/papers/LloydWAMCA18.pdf
14. Mokhtari, R., Stumm, M.: Bigkernel – high performance CPU-GPU communication pipelining for big data-style applications. In: International Parallel and Distributed Processing Symposium IPDPS, Phoenix, AZ, USA, pp. 819–828 (2014)
15. Oh, Y., et al.: APRES: improving cache efficiency by exploiting load characteristics on GPUs. ACM SIGARCH Comput. Archit. News **44**(3), 191–203 (2016)
16. Rau, B.R.: Iterative modulo scheduling: an algorithm for software pipelining loops. In: Proceedings of the 27th Annual International Symposium on Microarchitecture, MICRO 27, New York, NY, USA, pp. 63–74. ACM (1994)
17. Sethia, A., Jamshidi, D.A., Mahlke, S.: Mascar: speeding up GPU warps by reducing memory pitstops. In: High Performance Computer Architecture HPCA, San Francisco, CA, USA, pp. 174–185 (2015)
18. Sethia, A., Mahlke, S.: Equalizer: dynamic tuning of GPU resources for efficient execution. In: International Symposium on Microarchitecture MICRO, Cambridge, UK, pp. 647–658 (2014)

A Case Study for Performance Portability Using OpenMP 4.5

Rahulkumar Gayatri$^{(\boxtimes)}$, Charlene Yang, Thorsten Kurth, and Jack Deslippe

National Energy Research Scientific Computing Center (NERSC),
Lawrence Berkeley National Laboratory (LBNL), Berkeley, CA, USA
{rgayatri,cjyang,tkurth,jrdeslippe}@lbl.gov

Abstract. In recent years, the HPC landscape has shifted away from traditional multi-core CPU systems to energy-efficient architectures, such as many-core CPUs and accelerators like GPUs, to achieve high performance. The goal of performance portability is to enable developers to rapidly produce applications which can run efficiently on a variety of these architectures, with little to no architecture specific code adoptions required. We implement a key kernel from a material science application using OpenMP 3.0, OpenMP 4.5, OpenACC, and CUDA on Intel architectures, Xeon and Xeon Phi, and NVIDIA GPUs, P100 and V100. We will compare the performance of the OpenMP 4.5 implementation with that of the more architecture-specific implementations, examine the performance of the OpenMP 4.5 implementation on CPUs after backporting, and share our experience optimizing large reduction loops, as well as discuss the latest compiler status for OpenMP 4.5 and OpenACC.

Keywords: OpenMP 3.0 · OpenMP 4.5 · OpenACC · CUDA ·
Parallel programming models · P100 · V100 · Xeon Phi · Haswell

1 Introduction

The TOP500 list [1] is dominated by systems that employ accelerators and energy-efficient architectures in order to reach their quoted performance numbers. This trend is expected to continue and intensify on the road to exascale, and has increased the emphasis on "X" in "MPI + X", where "X" is an on-node programming framework, which allows for code parallelization over threads and/or vector lanes of a CPU and an accelerator. While "MPI" has established itself as the preferred choice for distributed programming by many, there is not yet a consensus choice for the on-node programming model. There are several options for "X" and they can be loosely categorized into the following.

1. Directive based approaches such as OpenMP, and OpenACC.
2. Architecture specific approaches such as POSIX Threads (pthreads), and CUDA.
3. Abstraction layers of data/task parallelism such as Intel Thread Building Blocks (TBB), OpenCL, Kokkos [2], and Raja [3].

© Springer Nature Switzerland AG 2019
S. Chandrasekaran et al. (Eds.): WACCPD 2018 Workshop, LNCS 11381, pp. 75–95, 2019.
https://doi.org/10.1007/978-3-030-12274-4_4

Architecture specific programming models usually require significant code changes and development efforts. The approach of using an abstraction layer for data/task parallelism on the other hand can add an extra dependency to the code. These models also commonly only support C/C++. In this paper, we focus on the viability of directive based on-node programming models, OpenMP in particular, with performance portability in mind.

OpenMP has been a prevailing programming model for years, especially for first time HPC programmers. Its ease of use and support from major compiler vendors has aided in its adoption as the first step in the parallelization of a sequential code. With version 4.0/4.5, the OpenMP standard has been extended to include support for accelerators. This means that one of the widely used programming models can now support parallelization over heterogeneous architectures via a single framework. That said, the implementation of OpenMP 4.5 by compiler vendors is still at an early stage, which we will have a close look at in this paper.

We investigate porting a relatively simple material science kernel that has been optimized on CPUs using OpenMP 3.0 [7]. We then implement it using OpenMP 4.5 [8] on the GPUs. We will compare the performance of the OpenMP 4.5 implementation with that of its OpenACC [9] counterpart, in terms of their kernel generation capabilities such as registers used and data moved, when different grid and thread dimensions are configured. We will discuss the challenges we faced when implementing the kernel with these frameworks and the techniques we used to improve the performance of each implementation. After an examination of our GPU implementations, we will discuss the performance of the GPU code back on the CPUs and provide an analysis of how portable and more specifically, performance portable it is.

Overall, this paper is structured around the discussions of

1. The optimization strategies for writing OpenMP 3.0/4.5 codes on CPU
2. Early experiences of OpenMP 4.5 on GPUs compared to other options
3. The portability of OpenMP 4.5 codes back on CPU,

with a goal that is two-fold:

1. To demonstrate that a single code can run across multiple (CPU and GPU) architectures using OpenMP 4.5, and
2. To demonstrate that such a code can give an acceptable level of performance compared to the optimized architecture-specific implementations.

The platforms we run on are: the Cori supercomputer [15] at the National Energy Research Scientific Computing Center (NERSC), Lawrence Berkeley National Laboratory (LBNL), for its Intel Haswell and Xeon Phi (Knights Landing (KNL)) architectures, and the Summit supercomputer [16] and the Summit-dev testbed at the Oak Ridge Leadership Computing Facility (OLCF), Oak Ridge National Laboratory (ORNL), for their NVIDIA P100 and V100 GPUs, as well as Power CPUs. At the time of writing, **xlc** and **xlc++** from IBM, **gcc** and **clang/llvm** are the primary compilers which support GPU offloading via

OpenMP 4.5 directives on these systems, and we have experimented with all the available compilers. For OpenACC, the compilers we used are from PGI, the **pgc** and **pgc++** compilers. The rest of the paper is organized as follows, Sect. 2 presents a basic introduction of the kernel and the application from which the kernel was extracted. In the same Section, from Subsect. 2.2, we present a baseline CPU implementation of the kernel which we will use as a reference for our GPU implementation. Section 3 presents our GPU implementations. In this Section, we will present our experiences with OpenMP4.5 directives and their effective use to optimize performance on a GPU. We compare our OpenMP implementation for GPUs with OpenACC and CUDA. In Sect. 4 we discuss our efforts in porting the GPU implementations back to the CPU. In Sect. 6, we talk about our final conclusions and plans for the future.

2   The GPP Kernel and Its Baseline CPU Implementation

In this section, we will introduce the General Plasmon Pole (GPP) kernel [6], which is a mini-application representing a single MPI rank's work extracted from a material science code BerkeleyGW [4,5]. BerkeleyGW itself can be used to compute the excited state properties of complex materials and its main computational bottlenecks are FFTs, dense linear algebra and large reductions, out of which, large reductions can take up 30% of the whole runtime for certain common execution paths. GPP represents the node level work of one of these reductions, and if optimized, can bring significant benefit to the performance of the whole code.

2.1   GPP Kernel

The GPP kernel computes the electron self-energy using the General Plasmon Pole approximation. Listing 1.1 shows the most basic pseudo code of this kernel in C++.

Listing 1.1. GPP pseudo code

```
1  for(X){         // X = 512
2      for(N){     // N = 32768/20
3          for(M){ // M = 32768
4              for(int iw = 0; iw < 3; ++iw){
5                  Some computation
6                  output[iw] += ...
7              }
8          }
9      }
10 }
```

The code was originally written in FORTRAN and employs OpenMP for on-node parallelization. However, in order to apply a large variety of performance portable programming approaches, we created a C++ port for the kernel.

The main computational work in the kernel is to perform a series of tensor-contraction-like operations (involving a non-trivial series of multiply, add and divide instructions) for a number of pre-computed complex double-precision arrays, and eventually reduce them to a small 3×3 matrix. The code uses a double-complex number as its primary data type. The problem discussed in this paper consists of 512 electrons and 32768 plane wave basis vectors and corresponds to a medium sized molecule such as Chlorophyll or a small piece of a surface. This choice of size leads to the following characteristics for the kernel:

1. The overall memory footprint is around 2 GB.
2. The first and second loop are closely nested and can be collapsed, with a resultant trip count of $\mathcal{O}(800K)$, which could be a target for thread parallelization on the CPUs or threadblock distribution on the GPUs.
3. The third loop has a fairly large trip count too and can be vectorized on the CPUs or parallelized with the threads within a threadblock on the GPUs.
4. The innermost loop has a small, fixed trip count and can be unrolled to facilitate SIMD/SIMT parallelization.

Despite the apparent simplicity, this kernel has a set of very interesting characteristics. For example, the reduction over a series of double-complex arrays that involves multiply add and divide instructions, which are left out of the paper to simplify the discussion. Also, the innermost iw loop has significant data-reuse potential whose dimension is problem size dependent (fixed as 3 for our purposes in this paper). For typical calculations, this leads to an arithmetic intensity of the kernel which is between 1–10, which implies that the kernel has to be optimized for both memory locality as well as thread and vectororization efficiency.

2.2   Baseline CPU Implementation

The shared memory parallel programming framework OpenMP [7] is a very attractive option for incremental parallelization of codes due to its ease of use and extensive support from compilers. To explicitly address parallelism on hardware of contemporary CPUs, the least version required is OpenMP 3.0, which supports common parallelization paradigms such as vectorization and code transformation features such as loop collapsing, but not the offloading features as in OpenMP 4.x.

Listing 1.2 shows our initial implementation of GPP on CPUs, using OpenMP 3.0, where we spread the "X" loop over threads and "M" loop over SIMD vector lanes. As written, vectorization is automatic by the Intel compiler, without any use of a pragma because the compiler chooses to fully unroll the inermost iw loop. In the general case it is necessary to insert an omp simd pragma outside the M loop. To represent a complex number, we built an in-house customized complex class that mimics the thrust-complex class available in the CUDA [17] framework.

Complex number reduction is not supported by OpenMP in C/C++ (but it is in Fortran). To work around this, we divide the output array into two separate data structures, output_re[3] and output_im[3], for their respective real and imaginary components, and apply reduction to these data structures. We could potentially have utilized a user defined reduction but experienced performance issues from certain compilers in the past. In cases where compilers do not support array reduction, we split the arrays into 6 real-number reductions.

Listing 1.2. GPP + OpenMP 3.0 for CPU

```
1   #pragma omp parallel for
2       reduction(+:output_re[0:3], output_im[0:3])
3   for(X){
4       for(N){
5           for(M){
6               for(int iw = 0; iw < 3; ++iw){
7                   //Compute and Store in local variables
8               }
9           }
10          for(int iw = 0; iw < 3; ++iw){
11              output_re[iw] += ...
12              output_im[iw] += ...
13          }
14      }
15  }
```

We execute the code in Listing 1.2 on IBM Power 8 [12], Power 9 [13] and on Intel Haswell [11] and Xeon Phi [10] architectures. As shown in Fig. 1, there is a significant performance difference on the Power processors and Intel architectures. While Power-9 performance is not the focus of this paper, we are investigating the performance gap with Haswell. Our Xeon- Phi timings for GPP is approximately 2.5 s and we use this number as a reference benchmark when porting the application to GPUs.

3   GPU Implementations of the GPP Kernel

A GPU consists of thousands of cores and they can be abstracted into two layers of parallelization from a programmer's point of view, thread blocks and threads. Thread blocks can form a 1D, 2D or 3D grid, each consisting of the same number of threads within the block. From a hardware perspective, the threads in a thread blocks are also grouped into warps of 32 threads, all executing the same instruction at any time (Volta supports independent thread scheduling). Several warps constitute a thread block, several thread blocks are assigned to a streaming multiprocessor (SM), and several tens of SMs make up the whole GPU card. Given the massive parallelism available, it is the programmer's responsibility to match the appropriate data or task parallelism in the code onto the thread blocks or threads within a block on the hardware, in order to take full advantage of the compute power of the card.

We will investigate three programming models on the GPU in this section, OpenMP 4.5, OpenACC and CUDA, with a focus on OpenMP 4.5. We will lay

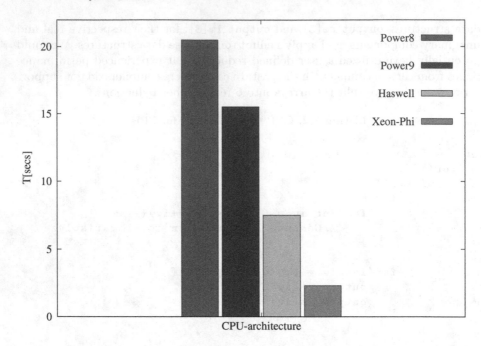

Fig. 1. Performance of GPP on multicores

out the compilation configurations and implementation details of GPP using these models, and will also compare them on aspects such as code generation capability, ease of use, compiler support, and code performance.

3.1 Implementation Groundwork

In this subsection we describe the settings and software used for compiling and running the GPP kernel. On the Summitdev system only **gcc** and **xl** compilers support accelerator offloading via OpenMP 4.5 (recent versions of clang were not tested), and the compilation flags used for these compilers are shown in Listing 1.3, Listing 1.4 and Listing ?? respectively.

Listing 1.3. Compile flags for **gcc** for OpenMP offloading

```
1  CXXFLAGS  = -g -O3 -std=c++11 -fopenmp
2  CXXFLAGS += -foffload=nvptx-none
3  LINKFLAGS = -fopenmp -foffload=nvptx-none
```

Listing 1.4. Compile flags for **xlc** for OpenMP offloading

```
1  CXXFLAGS=-O3 -std=gnu++11 -g -qsmp=noauto:omp
2  CXXFLAGS+=-qoffload #offload target regions to a GPU
3  CXXFLAGS+=-Xptxas -v #generate report, a CUDA flag
4  LINKFLAGS+=-qsmp=noauto #disable auto parallelization
5  LINKFLAGS+=-qsmp=omp -qoffload
```

In our experiments, we observed that the performance of kernels generated by **gcc** compiler was considerably worse than that of the **xl** compilers. Therefore, if not otherwise stated, we will use **xl/20180223-beta** and **xl/20180502** on Summitdev and Summit respectively for all OpenMP 4.5 enabled GPU offloading experiments in this paper. For OpenACC offloading, we employed version 18.4 of the **pgi** compiler available on Cori, SummitDev and Summit machines. **pgi** compile flags for Summitdev and Summit are shown in Listing 1.5.

Listing 1.5. Compile flags for **pgi** for OpenACC offloading

```
1  CXXFLAGS  = -fast -std=c++11 --gnu_extensions -Munroll
2  CXXFLAGS += -acc -ta=tesla:cc70 #CUDA kernels for V100
3  #CXXFLAGS += -acc -ta=tesla:cc60 #CUDA kernels for P100
4  CXXFLAGS += -Minfo=accel #generate report
5  LINKFLAGS = -acc -ta=tesla:cc70
6  #LINKFLAGS = -acc -ta=tesla:cc60
```

3.2 OpenMP 4.5

In order to map the GPP kernel efficiently to the GPU, we need to exploit the different levels of hardware parallelism described above. More precisely, we want to distribute the X, N and M loops across threadblocks and threads within a block in a way that it takes the maximum advantage of the available GPU resources.

In our initial experiments, as a naive CPU parallel programmer, we followed the idea of distributing X loop of Listing 1.1 across threadblocks and the N, M loops across threads within a threadblock. This is shown in Listing 1.6.

Listing 1.6. GPP with OpenMP 4.5 directives

```
1  #pragma omp target teams distribute
2      map(to:..) map(from:output_re[0:3],output_im[0:3])
3  for(X){
4      #pragma omp parallel for
5      for(N){
6          for(M){
7              for(int iw = 0; iw < 3; ++iw){
8                  //Store in local variables
9              }
10         }
11         for(int iw = 0; iw < 3; ++iw){
12             #pragma omp atomic
13             output_re[iw] += ...
14             #pragma omp atomic
15             output_im[iw] += ...
16         }
17     }
18 }
```

The **target** directive on line 1 offloads the code block that follows the directive onto the accelerator. The **teams distribute** directives divide the loop iterations into teams and distribute them among the threadblocks. The **parallel for** on line 4 will distribute the loop among the threads within a threadblock. We inline all function calls from inside the kernel region to avoid additional overhead caused by kernel calls from the device. Array reductions are not supported inside **target** regions by the **xl** compilers and therefore we resorted to our atomic update approach. We furthermore need to manage the data accessed inside the target region. This information is passed to the framework via the **map** clauses and their use is shown in Listing 1.6:

- **map(to:input[0:N])** - copy the values in the data structure to the device at the start of the **target** region.
- **map(tofrom:input-output[0:N])** - copy the values in the data structure to-and-from the device
- **map(from:output[0:N])** - copy the values in the data structure from the device at the end of the **target** region
- **map(alloc:input[0:N])** - A corresponding storage space for **input** is created on the device
- **map(delete:input[0:N])** - Delete the allocated data on the device

Our initial implementation shown in Listing 1.6 did not make the optimal use of available resources. It generated a kernel with 1280 threadblocks and 354 threads per block. Even though the X loop has only 512 iteration space, **xl** implementation of OpenMP 4.5 directives generated approximately twice the necessary threadblocks. The **xl** compilers distributed the N loop following the **parallel for** directive among the threads of a threadblock. Based on the iteration space and assuming all iterations take similar runtime, every thread would execute 4 iterations of the N loop and in every iteration the M loop is executed sequentially. This implies that the 3rd loop which has an iteration space of O(33K) are not parallelized. After experimentation with different combinations of work distribution Listing 1.7 shows our best implementation (without replacing atomic) of GPP.

Listing 1.7. Optimized GPP with OpenMP 4.5 with atomic

```
1   #pragma omp target enter data map(alloc:input[0:X]))
2   #pragma omp target teams distribute parallel for collapse(2)
3   map(tofrom:output_re[0:3], output_im[0:3])
4   for(X){
5       for(N){
6           for(M){
7               for(int iw = 0; iw < 3; ++iw){
8                   //Store in local variables
9                   }
10          }
11          #pragma omp atomic
12          output_re* += ...
13          #pragma omp atomic
14          output_im* += ...
15      }
16  #pragma omp target exit data map(delete:input[0:X]))
17  }
```

OpenMP provides clauses (`alloc`) to allocate data on the device. As mentioned in Sect. 2, the memory usage of GPP is approximately 2 GB and hence we can allocate all the necessary data on the device. The use of this clause improved the performance of the kernel by 10%, however, the total runtime of the application remained constant. This implies that prior to the usage of `alloc` clause, the kernel time evaluated also included the time taken for data transfers.

In Listing 1.7, we collapse the outer two loops and distribute the resulting iterations among threadblocks and threads within a block. This generates 6552 threadblocks and 128 threads per block. Even in this case all the iterations in the M loop are run sequentially by each thread. Distributing them among threads for parallelization increases the number of `atomic` updates relative to the loop iteration space i.e., $\mathcal{O}(33K)$. The benefits of parallelizing the M loop are overshadowed by the overhead incurred due to `atomic` updates which are necessary to maintain correctness.

To avoid the use of `atomic` and take advantage of parallelizing the M loop, we assign scalar variables to each of the three real and three imaginary components of `output` and pass them into the `reduction` clause. This optimization gave us a performance boost of 3×. `output_re*` and `output_im*` in Listing 1.8 represent these variables.

Listing 1.8. GPP + OpenMP 4.5 with **reduction** for GPU

```
1    #pragma omp target enter data map(alloc:input[0:X])
2    #pragma omp target teams distribute parallel for collapse(2)
3        reduction(+:output_re*, output_im*)
4    for(X){
5        for(N){
6            #pragma omp parallel for
7            reduction(+:output_re*, output_im*)
8            for(M){
9                for(int iw = 0; iw < 3; ++iw){
10                   //Store in local variables
11               }
12
13               output_re* += ...
14               output_im* += ...
15           }
16
17       }
18   #pragma omp target exit data map(delete:input[0:X])
19   }
```

Listing 1.8 shows the pseudo code for our most optimized implementation of GPP via OpenMP 4.5 directives. In this code we collapse the outer two loops, i.e., X and N and distribute them over threadblocks while the M loop is parallelized over the threads in a thread block. Since the values are updated inside the M loop we have a `reduction` clause with the `teams distribute` and `parallel for` directives. Unlike Listing 1.6 where `output_re` and `output_im` are passed to the `map(from:...)` clause, variables passed into the `reduction` clause need not be passed in any other clauses in the same directive. Listing 1.8 generates 1280 threadblocks and 512 threads per block. OpenMP 4.5 also provides clauses to control the grid and thread dimension generated by the framework. A programmer can use `num_teams` and `thread_limit` clauses to inform the framework about the number of threadblocks and threads per block with which the CUDA kernel should be launched. In our case we realized that the default kernel dimensions chosen by the compiler were optimal. Figure 2 shows the performance comparison between `atomic` and `reduction` on P100 and V100. Both the implementations use different parallelization techniques as shown in Listings 1.7 and 1.8 respectively. This implies that the use of `atomic` or `reduction` with **xl** compilers to maintain correctness might lead to different optimal parallelization strategies on a GPU.

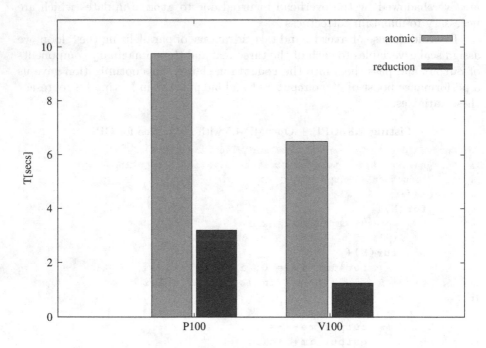

Fig. 2. `atomic` vs. `reduction` clauses for OpenMP 4.5 directives on P100 GPU.

xl vs gcc Implementation of OpenMP 4.5. Although, in the discussion above and for the rest of the paper, we focus on **xl** implementation of OpenMP 4.5, we were also successful in porting GPP with **gcc** compiler using the accelerator directives. In this section we present three major differences between the compiler implementations of OpenMP 4.5 directives that complicated the use of OpenMP 4.5 when targetting a code that is intended to support multiple compilers.

1. `simd` in the case of **xl** compilers is optional but mandatory for **gcc** to make use of all the threads in a warp.

2. The use of `map` clauses is mandatory for **xl** compilers. Every memory location accessed inside `target` region has to pass through one of the directionality clauses. In case of **gcc**, this condition is not enforced.
3. In practice it has been our observation that dynamic allocation of data structures inside the `target` directives fail with the **xl** compilers. This constraint is not applicable to **gcc** compilers.

3.3   OpenACC

Similar to OpenMP 4.5, OpenACC has its own directives to distribute loops across the threads of a GPU. OpenACC directives for work distribution across GPU threadblock and threads are **gang** and **vector** respectively.

The experiences gained in OpenMP offloading experiments helped us in tuning the OpenACC implementations. The best performance of GPP with OpenACC directives was achieved with the **reduction** implementation of OpenACC, similar to OpenMP 4.5 as shown in Listing 1.9.

Listing 1.9. GPP + OpenACC for GPU

```
1    #pragma enter data create(input[0:X]))
2    #pragma acc parallel loop gang collapse(2)
3        present(input[0:X]))
4        reduction(+:output_re*, output_im*)
5    for(X){
6        for(N){
7        #pragma acc loop vector\
8        #reduction(+:output_re*, output_im*)
9            for(M){
10               for(int iw = 0; iw < 3; ++iw){
11                   //Store in local variables
12                   }
13           }
14           output_re* += ...
15           output_im* += ...
16       }
17   #pragma exit data delete(input[0:X])
18   }
```

In Listing 1.9, the directives in line 2 collapse the X and N loop and distribute them among the threadblocks, while the directives in line 7 distribute the M loop among the threads in a threadblock.

The **reduction** versions of OpenACC and OpenMP 4.5 give equivalent performance. However the **pgi** compiler generates 65535 threadblocks and 128 threads per block for this parallelization which is significantly different than the 1280 threadblocks and 512 threads per block generated by the **xl** compiler in response to the OpenMP offload directives. Section 3.5 discusses the reasons for similar performance with different kernel configuration in greater detail.

The optimal **atomic** version with OpenACC occurs when we distribute the X loop among the threadblocks and N loop among the threads per block. For this version the compiler generated a kernel with 512 threadblocks and 128 threads per block and its performance is 2× faster than the atomic version of OpenMP 4.5. However, when we back-ported these changes to the **xl** implementations of OpenMP 4.5, we were unable to replicate the performance.

Line 1 and line 15 of Listing 1.9. are the data allocation directives of OpenACC. The **present** directive in line 3 informs the compiler that the data passed to this clause is available on the device. Otherwise **copyin** and **copyout** clauses are necessary to map the necessary data on-to the device. During our OpenACC implementation, we learned that the **pgi** compiler does not copy the data on to the device when encountered with the **data create** directives. The actual copy occurs when the corresponding data is encountered inside the kernel. In order to overcome this issue, we initialized the data on the device to guarantee its availability during kernel launch. This optimization was performed in order to avoid the inclusion of memory transfer time in kernel computation timing.

Figure 3 shows the comparison of atomic versus reduction versions of GPP on both the GPU architectures. The atomic version in the case of OpenACC is only 5% slower than the **reduction** version which is significantly lower than the difference between similar implementations of OpenMP 4.5.

3.4   CUDA

CUDA [17] is an extension of the C and C++ programming language, developed by NVIDIA to offload parallel kernels onto a GPU. We implemented 2 versions

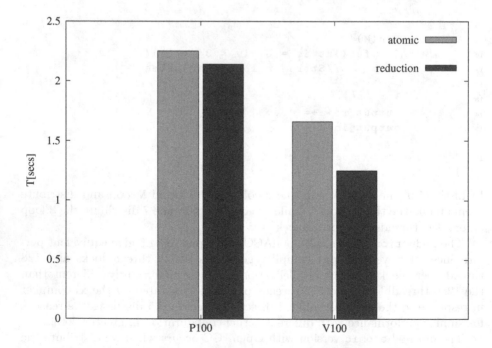

Fig. 3. atomic versus reduction in OpenACC on P100 and V100

of CUDA implementations for GPP which mimic the `atomic` and `reduction` versions of the OpenMP 4.5 implementation. In version 1, we implement a single dimension grid with the X loop being distributed across the threadblocks and N loop between the threads of a threadblock. In version 2 we generate a two dimensional grid. The 1st dimension is the outermost X loop and 2nd dimension is the N loop. The innermost M loop is distributed among the threads of a threadblock. Both the kernel launch parameters are shown in Listing 1.10.

Listing 1.10. Kernel parameters for CUDA version 1 and version 2

```
1  dim3 numBlocks(X,1,1);
2  dim3 numThreadsPerBlock(64,1,1);
3
4  //Version 2
5  dim3 numBlocks(X,N,1);
6  dim3 numThreadsPerBlock(32,1,1);
7
8  //Kernel Launch
9  gpp_Kernel<<<numBlocks, numThreadsPerBlock>>> (...);
```

We launch the kernels with 64 and 32 threads per threadblock for version 1 and version 2 respectively. In our experiments these proved to be the ideal kernel launch parameters for the respective versions. We use the `atomcAdd` routine in CUDA to maintain correctness of our updates.

While version 1 gave similar performance as the corresponding OpenACC `atomic` implementation, version 2 was approximately 2× faster compared to version 1. But as shown in Fig. 3, the difference between the `atomic` and `reduction` implementations of OpenACC was only 5%. This shows that the benefits of CUDA version 2 implementation were unavailable in the corresponding OpenACC or the OpenMP 4.5 versions which give similar performance.

3.5 Performance Comparison Among GPU Implementations

In this section we perform a detailed comparison among the available GPU implementations. We specifically focus on the differences between OpenMP 4.5 and OpenACC implementations of GPP and also the difference between compiler based implementations and architecture specific CUDA implementation.

OpenMP 4.5 vs OpenACC. As mentioned earlier our optimized OpenMP and OpenACC implementations have the same parallelization strategies Table 1 presents a comparison of the kernels generated by both these versions. Collapsing of X and N loops generates $\mathcal{O}(800K)$ iterations that can be distributed across the available threadblocks. From the details presented in Table 1, we observe that even though OpenACC generates 50× more threadblocks (and 4x fewer threads per block) than OpenMP, both the frameworks give us approximately the same runtime. Volta has 80 SMs at the hardware level on which the threadblocks can be scheduled. This implies that any kernel that generates more than 80 threadblocks has the additional threadblocks in the virtual space until their execution is scheduled on an SM. Hence having 50× more threadblocks might not translate into huge performance gains for the OpenACC implementation. Also having higher number of threads will lead to lower number of registers that can be allocated per thread which might effect the performance of the application.

Table 1. OpenACC vs OpenMP 4.5 kernel configuration on V100 reduction version

V100	Runtime	Grid-dim	Thread-dim	Registers
OpenACC(pgi/18.4)	1.24 s	(65535,1,1)	(128,1,1)	136
OpenMP(xlc/20180502)	1.25 s	(1280,1,1)	(512,1,1)	114

A summary of the hardware metrics and their comparison is shown in Table 2. While dram-utilization and warp-efficiency in both the implementations are similar, OpenMP has a 30% higher global-hit-rate, i.e., hit rate for global load and store in L1 cache and a somewhat higher occupancy, i.e., the ratio of active warps to the maximum number of warps per cycle. We expect on OpenACC the latency of the misses is effectively hidden by the additional overall threads available and there is a high enough arithmetic intensity to avoid saturating memory bandwidth. This implies that while both the versions give similar performance, their use of hardware resources are significantly different.

GPP Performance on Contemporary GPUs. In this section we perform a general comparison among all the available GPU implementations of the kernel. The horizontal dash line in Fig. 4 represents the performance of GPP on Xeon Phi against which we compare our GPU implementations. As observed the Fig. 4, apart from the OpenMP 4.5 version on P100, all other implementations perform better than OpenMP 3.0 implementation on Xeon Phi. OpenMP 4.5 in particular, shows a drastic improvement in its performance relative to other implementations on Volta compared to Pascal. The main reason for this is the use of a new compiler on the Summit machine, which is unavailable on Summitdev. This shows the importance of compiler maturity in generating optimal CUDA kernels via the offload directives.

An important observation in Fig. 4 is the approximately 2× difference between P100 and V100 performance. We also want to assert that the code implementations were consistent for every framework on both the GPUs. Further investigation is required but we are initially attributing the faster performance

Table 2. OpenACC vs OpenMP 4.5 kernel configuration on V100 reduction version

V100	Dram-utilization	Global-hit-rate	Warp-efficiency	Occupancy
OpenACC(pgi/18.4)	8 (high)	54.05%	99.92%	0.19
OpenMP(xlc/20180502)	7 (high)	84.6	99.86%	0.27

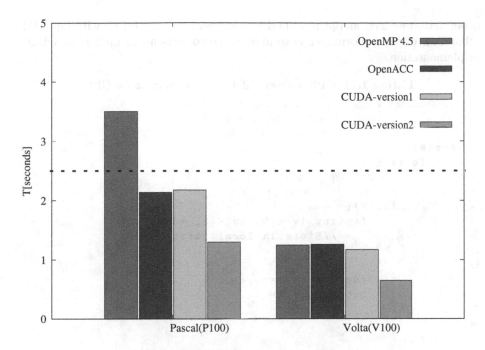

Fig. 4. Performance on P100 and V100

on Volta GPU to the following: (1) Compared to Pascal, Volta has a bigger and faster L1 cache; (2) global atomic is 2× faster, which may be important for reductions in GPP; (3) lower instruction latency.

As mentioned in Sect. 3.4, our CUDA version 2 implementation of GPP is similar to the **reduction** version of OpenMP and OpenACC, however its runtime is approximately 2× faster. The reason for this is the order in which the **X** and **Y** dimensions of the grid are assigned by OpenMP and OpenACC implementations. The optimized CUDA implementation, i.e., the version 2, assigns the N-loop to **Y** dimension and X-loop to **X** dimension of the grid, as shown in Listing 1.10. Both the **xl** and **clang** implementations of OpenMP and **pgi** implementation of OpenACC assign the **X** dimension of the grid to the innermost loop during a collapse. Hence in an effort to make OpenMP and OpenACC implementations more similar to the optimized CUDA implementation, we swapped the outer two loops as shown in Listing 1.11.

The code change that is shown in Listing 1.11 gave a 2× benefit in the performance in case of OpenMP. Similar change to the OpenACC implementation, improved it's performance by 30%. These results are shown in Fig. 5. Unfortunately we could not test out final optimization's on P100 since the compiler versions used for the OpenMP implementations on Summitdev are no longer available. As shown in Fig. 5, Summit also has a clang compiler which supports OpenMP offloading. From the results shown in Fig. 5, we can observe that we have an optimized GPP implementation for GPUs with OpenMP offloading whose performance is similar to the corresponding optimized CUDA implementation.

Listing 1.11. GPP + OpenMP 4.5 with `reduction` for GPU

```
1   #pragma omp target enter data map(alloc:input[0:X])
2   #pragma omp target teams distribute parallel for collapse(2)
3       reduction(+:output_re*, output_im*)
4   for(N){
5       for(X){
6           #pragma omp parallel for
7           reduction(+:output_re*, output_im*)
8           for(M){
9               for(int iw = 0; iw < 3; ++iw){
10                  //Store in local variables
11                  }
12
13                  output_re* += ...
14                  output_im* += ...
15          }
16
17      }
18  #pragma omp target exit data map(delete:input[0:X])
19  }
```

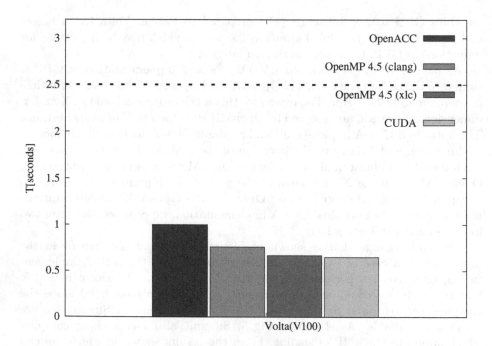

Fig. 5. Optimized performance of GPU implementations

4 Porting GPU Implementations Back to CPU

As mentioned in Introduction of this paper, our aim is to evaluate the status of the current programming frameworks and their ability to create a single code implementation that can be executed across architectures. In this section we discuss the performance of OpenMP and OpenACC GPU implementations on CPUs, especially Intel's Haswell and Xeon Phi.

4.1 OpenACC

Initially, **pgi** compilers were unable to parallelize GPP loops annotated with OpenACC directives on CPUs. The compiler appeared to assume dependencies between variables declared inside the loops which should technically be considered thread-private. The **pgi** compiler as a part of its aggressive optimization hoists variables declared inside the loop. This implies that the OpenACC directives would annotate these variables as shared, if stated otherwise, and prevent the parallelization of these loops. To avoid these problems, we declared the said variables outside the loops and marked them **private** to avoid dependency assumptions by the compiler.

Even after the said changes, **pgi** compiler was unable to vectorize the code for CPUs. Hence OpenACC implementation on CPUs for GPP is 4× slower than the OpenMP implementation.

4.2 OpenMP 4.5

For the compilation of OpenMP 4.5 on Haswell and Xeon Phi, we used the `intel/18.0.1.163` compiler on the Cori machine. Listing 1.12, shows the flags used in order to compile the code on CPUs.

Listing 1.12. Intel flags for OpenMP 4.5

```
1    CXXFLAGS=-O3 -std=c++11 -qopenmp -qopt-report=5
2    CXXFLAGS+=-qopenmp-offload=host #For offloading
3    #CXXFLAGS+=-xCORE-AVX2 #For Haswell
4    CXXFLAGS+=-xMIC-AVX512 #For Xeon Phi
5    LINKFLAGS=-qopenmp
6    LINKFLAGS+=-qopenmp-offload=mic #For Xeon Phi
```

Intel compiler, when encountered the with the **target teams** directive of OpenMP 4.5 on a CPU, generates a single team and assigns all the threads available to the team. Hence when the corresponding **parallel for** is encountered, the loop following the directive is parallelized among the available threads. In case of our best OpenMP 4.5 **reduction** implementation, this translates to the outermost X and N being collapsed and run sequentially, while the innermost M loop is distributed among the threads. In the case of GPP, this interpretation of OpenMP offload directives lead to a "portable" but not "performance portable" code since such a parallelization increases the GPP runtime by 25× compared to the optimized OpenMP 3.0 implementation. In order to optimize

GPP with OpenMP 4.5 on CPUs, we modified the implementation by moving the `parallel for` directives on X loop as shown in Listing 1.13.

Listing 1.13. GPP + OpenMP 4.5 on CPU

```
1  #pragma omp target teams distribute parallel for
2      reduction(+:output_re*, output_im*)
3  for(X){
4      for(N){
5          for(M){
6              for(iw = 0; iw < 3; ++iw)
7                  {//Store in local variables}
8          }
9          output_re* += ...
10         output_im* += ...
11     }
12 }
```

This creates a team of 272 or 64 threads for Xeon Phi or Haswell and distributes the X loop across the available threads. This is similar to the OpenMP 3.0 implementation of GPP.

Figure 6 shows a comparison of executing optimal GPU and CPU implementations with OpenMP 4.5 directives on Xeon Phi and Volta. As can be observed the performance of CPU optimized OpenMP 4.5 implementation is similar to the

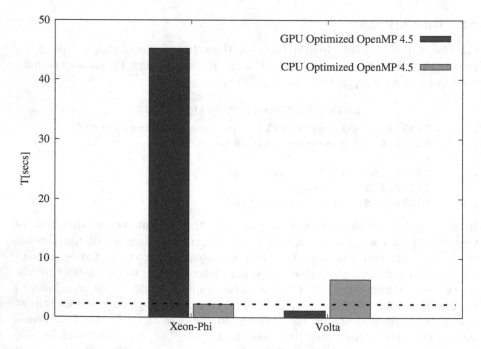

Fig. 6. OpenMP 4.5 on CPU

optimized OpenMP 3.0 runtime. However, on GPU the implementation is 5×
slower than the optimized OpenMP 4.5 implementation for GPUs. Conversely,
the optimized GPU implementation with OpenMP 4.5 is 25× slower than the
optimized implementation on Xeon Phi. This experiment shows that the assumption by the **intel** compilers where they equate the threads on a CPU and threads
in a GPU's threadblock did not result in a "performance portable" code in the
case of GPP.

5 Related Work

Since OpenMP 4.5 began gaining traction with compilers, there have been a
number studies performed in the community to compare its performance and cost
of implementation to other GPU programming models. Our effort is intended
to be complimentary to these published works, represent a specific case-study of
importance to the Material Science community and document a snapshot of the
current state of support under rapid OpenMP 4.5 development and optimization
over the past few years.

One of the early works to evaluate OpenMP 4.0 on Xeon Phi and GPUs is
published in [20]. In this they chose a kernel representative of regular workloads
on Titan and attempt to port it across widely used HPC architectures such
as CPU, CPU+accelerator and self hosted coprocessor using OpenMP 4.0. In
[19], the authors evaluate and analyze OpenMP 4.X benchmarks on Power8
and NVIDIA Tesla K80 platform. They perform an analysis of hand written
CUDA code and the automatic GPU code generated using IBM xl compilers
and clang/LLVM compilers from high level OpenMP 4.x programs. Our work
differs from the paper in two major areas: (1) The kernel we ported is more
complicated and uses a template class to represent a complex number, and; (2)
We back-port the GPU implementations of OpenMP 4.5 onto CPUs.

In [18], the authors evaluate the "state of the art" for achieving performance
portability using compiler directives. The paper performs an in-depth analysis
of the how OpenMP 4.0 model performs on K20X GPU and in Xeon Phi architectures for commonly used kernel such as "daxpy" and "dgemm". However
unlike this paper, they do not discuss the kernel configurations generated by the
frameworks and their impact on the various parallel-loops inside the kernel.

6 Summary and Future Work

In this paper, we presented an analysis on the effort needed to port a kernel onto
CPUs and GPUs using OpenMP in comparison to other approaches with focus
on OpenACC.

We were successful in porting our best implementation of OpenMP 4.5 onto
CPUs with some important changes to the implementation. The performance
of this version is equivalent to our best OpenMP 3.0 version. But, an exactly
unchanged OpenMP 4.5 version optimized for GPUs is ill-suited for CPU execution.

In the future we want to evaluate the practical amount of work required to port kernels which exceed the memory space that can be allocated on the device. Although there are plans to include UVM support from OpenMP 5 version, the xlc compilers allow passing of device pointers to the framework.

Acknowledgement. This research has used resources of the Oak Ridge Leadership Computing Facility and National Energy Research Scientific Computing Center (NERSC) which are supported by the Office of Science of the U.S. Department of Energy. While the use of the GPP kernel in this work was largely for exploration of performance portability strategies rather than of the kernel itself, JD acknowledges support for the discussions around BerkeleyGW and use of the GPP kernel from the Center for Computational Study of Excited-StatePhenomena in Energy Materials (C2SEPEM) which is funded by the U.S. Department of Energy, Office of Science, Basic Energy Sciences, MaterialsSciences and Engineering Division under Contract No. DE-AC02-05CH11231, as part of the Computational Materials Sciences Program.

A   Reproducibility

Due to the nature and the content of our work, we have included the information about the hardware and software frameworks associated with our results in the paper. The paper also includes the compilers used and the associated flags used for the results. Interested individuals can contact the authors if they need access to the github repository for the case study.

References

1. TOP500 Supercomputers list. https://www.top500.org/lists/2018/06/
2. Edwards, H.C., Trott, C.R., Sunderland, D.: Kokkos: enabling manycore performance portability through polymorphic memory access patterns. J. Parallel Distrib. Comput. **74**(12), 3202–3216 (2014)
3. Hornung, R.D., Keasler, J.A.: The RAJA poratability layer: overview and status. Tech report, LLNL-TR-661403, September 2014
4. Deslippe, J., Samsonidze, G., Strubbe, D.A., Jain, M., Cohen, M.L., Louie, S.G.: BerkeleyGW: a massively parallel computer package for the calculation of the quasiparticle and optical properties of materials and nanostructures. Comput. Phys. Commun. **183**(6), 1269–1289 (2012)
5. BerkeleyGW Code. https://berkeleygw.org
6. Soininen, J., Rehr, J., Shirley, E.: Electron self-energy calculation using a general multi-pole approximation. J. Phys.: Condens. Matter **15**(17) (2003)
7. https://www.openmp.org/
8. https://www.openmp.org/wp-content/uploads/OpenMP-4.5-1115-CPP-web.pdf
9. https://www.openacc.org/
10. Intel Knights Landing Processor. https://ark.intel.com/products/94034/Intel-Xeon-Phi-Processor-7230-16GB-1_30-GHz-64-cor
11. Intel Haswell Processor: Haswell: The Fourth-Generation Intel Core Processor. IEEE Micro **34**(2), 6–20 (2014)
12. Sinharoy, B., et al.: IBM POWER8 processor core microarchitecture. IBM J. Res. Dev. **59**(1), 2:1–2:21 (2015)

13. Sadasivam, S.K., Thompto, B.W., Kalla, R., Starke, W.J.: IBM Power9 processor architecture. IEEE Micro **37**(2), 40–51 (2017)
14. NVIDIA V100 GPU Whitepaper. http://images.nvidia.com/content/volta-architecture/pdf/volta-architecture-whitepaper.pdf
15. http://www.nersc.gov/users/computational-systems/cori/
16. https://www.olcf.ornl.gov/summit/
17. Nickolls, J., Buck, I., Garland, M., Skadron, K.: Scalable parallel programming with CUDA. Queue **6**(2), 40–53 (2008). https://doi.org/10.1145/1365490.1365500
18. Lopez, M.G., et al.: Towards achieving performance portability using directives for accelerators. In: 2016 Third Workshop on Accelerator Programming Using Directives (WACCPD) (2016)
19. Hayashi, A., Shirako, J., Tiotto, E., Ho, R., Sarkar, V.: Exploring compiler optimization opportunities for the OpenMP 4.× accelerator model on a POWER8+ GPU platform. In: 2016 Third Workshop on Accelerator Programming Using Directives (WACCPD) (2016)
20. Vergara, L.V.G., Wayne, J., Lopez, M.G., Hernández, O.: Early experiences writing performance portable OpenMP 4 codes. In: Proceedings of Cray User Group Meeting, London, England. Cray User Group Incorporated, May 2016

Program Evaluation

OpenACC Routine Directive Propagation Using Interprocedural Analysis

Aniket Shivam[1][(✉)] and Michael Wolfe[2]

[1] University of California, Irvine, CA, USA
aniketsh@uci.edu
[2] NVIDIA/PGI, Hillsboro, OR, USA
mwolfe@nvidia.com

Abstract. Accelerator programming today requires the programmer to specify what data to place in device memory, and what code to run on the accelerator device. When programming with OpenACC, directives and clauses are used to tell the compiler what data to copy to and from the device, and what code to compile for and run on the device. In particular, the programmer inserts directives around code regions, typically loops, to identify compute constructs to be compiled for and run on the device. If the compute construct calls a procedure, that procedure also needs to be marked for device compilation, as does any routine called in that procedure, and so on transitively. In addition, the marking needs to include the kind of parallelism that is exploited within the procedure, or within routines called by the procedure. When using separate compilation, the marking where the procedure is defined must be replicated in any file where it is called. This causes much frustration when first porting existing programs to GPU programming using OpenACC.

This paper presents an approach to partially automate this process. The approach relies on interprocedural analysis (IPA) to analyze OpenACC regions and procedure definitions, and to propagate the necessary information forward and backward across procedure calls spanning all the linked files, generating the required accelerator code through recompilation at link time. This approach can also perform correctness checks to prevent compilation or runtime errors. This method is implemented in the PGI OpenACC compiler.

Keywords: Automatic directive propagation ·
Interprocedural analysis (IPA) · OpenACC · GPU Computing

1 Introduction

Accelerator programming has been used for at least forty years. Accelerators are typically optimized for certain common program structures, often without the ability to run a whole program or to support a full operating system. They

---

A. Shivam—Work done at NVIDIA/PGI.

S. Chandrasekaran et al. (Eds.): WACCPD 2018 Workshop, LNCS 11381, pp. 99–113, 2019.
https://doi.org/10.1007/978-3-030-12274-4_5

are used when the program can be sped up by offloading the bulk of the computation to the accelerator, leaving the main program on the CPU to handle input/output and interaction with a user. Programming a typical accelerator-enabled machine requires the programmer to identify when to allocate space in device memory, when to copy data to and from system memory, and when to launch a computation on the device.

While early accelerators came with a set of preprogrammed libraries and procedures, current accelerators allow users to write their own programs. To do so, the user must identify what parts of the program need to be compiled for and run on the accelerator. One approach is to use a language or language extensions, such as CUDA C++ [8,11] or CUDA Fortran [15] for NVIDIA GPUs. With CUDA C++ or Fortran, the programmer explicitly allocates device memory, explicitly copies data between host and device, and explicitly launches *kernels*, which are specially written procedures that run in parallel on the GPU. OpenCL [13] is a similar programming model supported on a variety of devices, including GPUs.

The OpenACC Application Programming Interface (API) [2,9,12] is another parallel programming model that supports offloading parallel computations to accelerators, including NVIDIA and AMD GPUs. OpenACC uses directives in C++, C, and Fortran programs, similar to OpenMP [14], to tell the compiler what data to copy between system and device memory, and to mark the regions of code, typically loops, to run in parallel on the device. OpenACC has proved popular because it doesn't require a wholesale rewrite of the program, though many programs need restructuring to expose enough parallelism to fully exploit a GPU. OpenACC programs have three *levels* of parallelism, *gang*, *worker*, and *vector*. At the most coarse level, *gang* parallelism is used for fully parallel loops that need no synchronization or barriers beyond atomic operations and reductions; for GPU execution, iterations of a *gang* parallel loop can be mapped to CUDA thread blocks or OpenCL work groups. Within a gang, *worker* parallelism is used for parallel loops where the iterations may need to coordinate or synchronize; for GPU execution, iterations of a *worker* parallel loop can be mapped to groups of threads with a CUDA thread block (such as a warp), or groups of work items in an OpenCL work group. Within a worker, *vector* parallelism is used for SIMD operations or parallelism which is synchronous or mostly synchronous, and which is sensitive to memory strides; for GPU execution, iterations of a *vector* parallel loop are typically mapped to the *threadIdx.x* dimension of a CUDA thread block or dimension 0 of an OpenCL work group, to benefit from contiguous memory references. OpenACC programs can also be recompiled for host or multicore parallel execution, with gang and/or worker loops compiled for execution across the cores, and vector loops compiled for SIMD execution.

As more nontrivial programs were ported to GPUs using OpenACC, it became obvious that there needed to be a way to compile and run whole procedures on the device. Moreover, because of the way OpenACC parallelism on GPUs is commonly implemented, when there are parallel loops in the called procedure, both the caller and callee must know what level of parallelism is used in the called procedure. There were three options available for implementing this. One way would be to compile all procedures for GPU execution, just as all procedures are compiled for the host CPU. While this may become viable in the future, there are many operations that current GPUs just do not support, such as direct I/O, host memory management, and so on. Also, the compiler wouldn't necessarily know the level of parallelism used in a procedure that appears in another file.

Another way would be to have the compiler determine which procedures are called within a compute construct and compile those for the device as well. Transitively, the compiler would need to find all procedures called from any of those procedures and generate device code, and so on. This is straightforward for C or C++ within a single file, and in fact the PGI C++ compiler already implements this, though it doesn't propagate the level of parallelism in the procedure to the call site. This is a bit more problematic for Fortran, since Fortran doesn't have the concept of *file scope*, but that could be worked around.

A third way, and the way selected in OpenACC (and in the OpenMP 4.0 and 4.5 target directives) because it depends least on compiler technology, is to have the programmer mark the procedures needed on the device, along with the level of parallelism used within those procedures. This solution requires the most work from programmers, and has been the source of much frustration at various GPU Hackathons[1] when beginning users start to add OpenACC directives to an existing program. In OpenACC, the programmer must insert a `routine` directive for each procedure that must be compiled for the GPU where that procedure is defined. A procedure so marked is called a *device routine*, since it can be called on the device. If it is called from a different file, the programmer must insert a matching `routine` directive in that file (or in an appropriate header file). Fortran *modules* simplify this somewhat, since the necessary `routine` information is propagated through the normal Fortran module mechanism.

In current implementations, if a procedure call appears in an OpenACC compute construct or routine compiled for the device with no appropriate `routine` directive for that procedure, the compiler can either issue an error message, or assume that device code for that procedure will be provided. The latter case can result in a link-time error, if the procedure was not compiled for the device, and can result in a run-time error, if the level of parallelism assumed at the call site does not match the level of parallel expected in the called procedure.

The PGI compilers currently provide the most complete and mature implementation of OpenACC. They also support a comprehensive and extensible version of interprocedural analysis (IPA), or whole program optimization. In the PGI implementation, the compiler saves a both a brief *program summary* and complete *recompile information* in the generated object file. At link time, a fast interprocedural analyzer is invoked, which reads all the available program summary information. For files and libraries not built with the summary information, such as system libraries, IPA reads the symbol table from the object files or libraries. The summary information and symbol tables allow IPA to build

---

[1] https://www.olcf.ornl.gov/training-event/2017-gpu-hackathons/.

a complete call graph and propagate information both forward and backward through the graph. Files containing procedures that would benefit from IPA optimizations are then recompiled before the linker is invoked.

For this work, we explored using the PGI IPA facility to ease OpenACC programming, by adding or propagating OpenACC `routine` directives throughout an application at link time. This can detect and insert missing `routine` directives at call sites or at routine definitions, or detect errors when existing `routine` directives don't match. The IPA step then recompiles the files which contain either call sites or called procedures where new `routine` directives are inserted.

The remainder of the paper is organized as follows. Section 2 describes the OpenACC `routine` directive and the clauses. Section 3 describes our implementation. Section 4 describes cases where our implementation benefits OpenACC programmers. Section 5 summarizes our work and the benefits for the OpenACC programmers.

2   OpenACC Routine Directive

When a procedure call is encountered in an OpenACC compute region, the *callee* might be defined in the same C or C++ file or the same Fortran module, or might be (explicitly or implicitly) declared with a prototype or Fortran interface block. For each such *callee* procedure, to avoid compile-time and link-time errors, the user needs to tell the compiler to generate both host and accelerator code. This is done with the OpenACC `routine` directive. For C and C++, a `routine` directive should appear immediately before the definition of the function or its prototype. For Fortran, the `routine` directive should appear in the specification part of the subprogram or its interface block. Alternatively, a `routine` directive can specify a procedure name, and can then appear anywhere in a C or C++ file that a function prototype is allowed or in a Fortran specification part of a subprogram.

A `routine` directive has a list of clauses, including one required clause to specify the level of parallelism used in the routine. One of the following clauses must appear on any `routine` directive:

- `gang` clause, if the routine has a *gang*-parallel loop, or calls a routine with a *gang*-parallel loop.
- `worker` clause, if the routine has a *worker*-parallel loop, or calls a routine with a *worker*-parallel loop.
- `vector` clause, if the routine has a *vector*-parallel loop, or calls a routine vector a *vector*-parallel loop.
- `seq` clause, if the routine has no parallel loops and calls no routines with parallel loops.

There are other clauses (`bind`, `device_type` and `nohost`), but they are not related to this paper's contribution.

For procedures that are defined in one source file and called in a compute construct in other files, a `routine` directive must appear in the file where the

```
#pragma acc routine seq
extern float externfunc1( float );
...
void test( float* x, int n) {
    #pragma acc parallel loop copy(x[0:n])
    for( int i = 0; i < n; ++i )
        x[i] = externfunc1(x[i]);
}
```

(a) main.c

```
#pragma acc routine seq
float externfunc2( float* x ){
    return x%2;
}
...
#pragma acc routine seq
float externfunc1( float* x ){
    return externfunc2(x) + 1;
}
```

(b) external.c

Fig. 1. Function call for an external function inside a parallel loop of a OpenACC C program

procedure is defined, and another **routine** directive with the same level-of-parallelism clause must be included in each source file where the function is called. This requires training and additional programming effort for beginning OpenACC programmers, and can require significant effort and attention from users when porting, maintaining, and updating large applications to OpenACC. We intend to ease these restrictions in this work.

An example of how a OpenACC programmer must mark all the declarations and the definition for the function being called inside a parallel region in shown in Fig. 1. In the example, the parallel construct defined in the *test* function in *main.c* calls an external function called *externfunc1* defined in *external.c*. The declaration for *externfunc1* in *main.c* is marked with the OpenACC **routine** directive with the **seq** clause. The same OpenACC directive is also marked for the function in *external.c* where it is defined. Not doing so will lead to link time error, since the accelerator code for *externfunc1* would not be generated during compilation. In addition to this, *externfunc1* calls another function called *externfunc2* which needs to be marked with the **routine** directive as well and must be marked before its usage in *externfunc1*. If this function is not marked with **routine** directive then compiler will generate a compile time error at the call site, since it appears in the same file as the call site.

3 Implementation of Automatic Routine Directive Propagation

This section describes our implementation of OpenACC routine propagation using the PGI compiler Interprocedural Analysis (IPA) feature. The PGI IPA feature is described briefly in Sect. 3.1. Section 3.2 describes the modifications to the initial compile step, and in particular what information is gathered for IPA. The following subsections describe how IPA navigates the call graphs to determine what `routine` directives need to be added, and then what functions or files need to be recompiled. The final subsection briefly describes the recompile step.

3.1 PGI Interprocedural Analysis

The PGI IPA feature is based on the whole program analysis work done by researchers at Rice University [1,3–7,10]. It is divided into three distinct parts: the initial compile step, the link-time interprocedural analysis, and the recompile step, when necessary.

When compiling a file with the PGI compilers and IPA enabled (with the -Mipa flag), the compiler adds one additional analysis phase early in the compile sequence. This is the IPA *summary* phase, which saves a concise summary of each procedure and all the global variables in the program. The summary contains information such as:

- all procedures called, including indirect procedure calls, along with the arguments to those procedures
- what variables or procedures have had their addresses taken
- assignments to global variables or reference arguments
- loops in the procedure
- an estimate of the size and complexity of the procedure

This phase also saves *recompile* information, which includes the program intermediate representation as well as information such as the compiler flags used to build the object file, so the routines in this file can be recompiled without the source files or can be inlined into procedures in other files.

Unlike almost all other compilers with interprocedural analysis or whole program optimization, the PGI compiler then continues to produce a valid object file. That object file would obviously not be optimized with IPA, but otherwise is a valid object file that can be saved in an object library or linked without IPA. The IPA summary and recompile information is appended in special sections of the object file. This means that an object file compiled with IPA enabled can be linked with or without IPA. When linked without IPA, the generated program will not benefit from IPA, since it will be using the non-IPA-optimized object file, but there are no drawbacks.

The interprocedural analysis occurs at link time. When linking with IPA enabled, the PGI interprocedural analyzer is invoked before the linker itself.

The analyzer opens all the object files on the link line, looking for the IPA summary information saved there. It also opens object libraries, just like the linker, satisfying unresolved external references and looking for IPA summary information in the library objects.

For object files that don't have IPA summary information, the analyzer reads the object file symbol table and assumes *worst case* information. Any symbol defined in a worst-case object file that is called from another object file is assumed to be a procedure. Any symbol defined in a worst-case object file that is not called from another object is assumed to be a global variable. Any variable symbol referenced in a worst-case object file is assumed to be read and written, and to have its address taken, in any procedure defined in that object. Any procedure symbol referenced in a worst-case object file is assumed to be called from any procedure defined in that file.

The analyzer then builds a complete call graph, using the mechanism described by Cooper and Kennedy [6], along with the argument binding graph. The call graph nodes are the procedures, and edges represent the procedure caller to callee relationship. The argument binding graph nodes are variables, constants, and procedure dummy arguments, and the edges represent when a variable, constant, or a dummy argument is passed as a value or reference actual argument at a call site to a dummy argument. These are the main data structures used in the analyzer. Most IPA analyses requires one or a few traversals of these graphs, either forward or backward, to propagate information across the edges and make decisions about what optimizations may be performed.

When the analysis is complete, the IPA step decides what functions (and hence what files) to recompile. Because of the structures used, the PGI compiler will recompile whole object files. The analyzer reinvokes the compiler on those files, using the generated IPA information, to generate *optimized object files*. When all these recompilations are complete, the analyzer then invokes the system linker, substituting optimized object files on the link line, or adding optimized object files for any that were extracted from libraries.

There are a few engineering details to make the recompile step more efficient. When recompiling files at link time, IPA can do several recompiles at a time, much like make -j. Also, the optimized object files are not generally deleted, but saved with a .oo suffix. The interprocedural information that was used to optimize that file is appended as a special section to the optimized object. If the same program is rebuilt in that directory, and IPA sees an existing optimized object for a file, it will compare the dates for the original and optimized object file, and the interprocedural information that was used to generate the existing optimized object to the interprocedural information that it just generated. If the optimized object is stale (the original object file is newer), or the interprocedural information has changed, then the optimized object must be rebuilt.

3.2   Initial Compile Summary Information and Error Suppression

This subsection describes how we augmented the IPA summary information collection step for routine propagation. First, if a procedure was compiled for the device with an `acc routine` directive, the information for that directive is added to the summary information. Second, the summary information for a procedure calls includes whether it appears in an OpenACC compute construct or a procedure marked by a `routine` directive. Third, any information from `acc routine` directives for called procedures is also added to the summary information. Fourth, information about global variables is extended to include whether that variable appears in an `acc declare` directive.

Normally, a procedure call to a routine in an OpenACC compute construct or device routine that does not have appropriate `acc routine` information results in a compiler error message. Since our new method will implicitly generate or propagate the `routine` information at link time, we suppress these errors for the initial compile step. As mentioned in the previous subsection, the PGI IPA initial compile phase produces a complete object file. In this case, however, the object file cannot be complete, since the compiler can't determine what level of parallelism should be used for procedures without `routine` information. This is the most significant change in the compile workflow. If a user builds a program with this optimization enabled but then links without IPA, the program will fail to link.

3.3   Propagating `acc routine` Information with IPA

There are five small modifications to the interprocedural analysis to support `acc routine` propagation. These are all done with a single depth-first pass through the call graph. Indirect procedure calls (through a function pointer) are not handled. See the discussion on limitations in Sect. 5.

First, a procedure call in an OpenACC compute construct or in a device routine was so annotated in the summary information. This allows IPA to check whether the callee was already marked as a device routine. If not, IPA will mark it as an implicit device routine and recurse to any of its callees. Second, if the callee was marked as a device routine but the file containing the caller did not have that routine information, IPA will propagate that information to the callee. Third, if the callee is marked as a device routine with one parallelism level, but the caller had an `acc routine` directive for that routine with a different parallelism level, IPA will generate a fatal error message. Fourth, IPA will assign a parallelism level for any implicit device routine. Normally, IPA will treat any implicit device routine as `acc routine seq`. However, if this routine calls another routine with a higher parallelism level (gang > worker > vector > seq), the implicit device routine is assigned the highest parallelism level of all routines called.

During the call graph traversal, IPA checks for several types of errors, and issues fatal error messages if any are found. IPA checks that the call site is at the proper level of parallelism for the callee. For instance, a call within a gang-parallel loop cannot be made to a `routine gang` procedure, because gang-level parallelism was already exploited at the call site. IPA also checks that explicit `acc routine` information at each call site and procedure definition match. Finally, IPA checks that any global variable referenced in an implicit device routine has appeared in an `acc declare` directive. IPA can't implicitly insert an `acc` declare directive without also inserting data movement to keep the host and device copies of the global variable coherent, and that's a problem that we don't know how to solve at this point. However, it can and does propagate the acc declare from the definition site to any file where it is referenced in an OpenACC construct or a device routine.

3.4 Recompile Step

Assuming no errors were detected, IPA finishes by determining whether any new interprocedural information can be used to optimize any function in each object file. Implicit OpenACC routine information is one such type of information. As mentioned earlier, interprocedural optimizations are usually optional, as the existing initial compile generates a complete object file. In this case, the recompile is required, since the initial compile was made with inadequate information. IPA will create a description of the implicit acc routine information along with any other interprocedural optimization information, and reinvoke the compiler to reprocess any object file that needs to be recompiled. This might be because the object file contains a procedure that needs to be compiled with a new implicit acc routine directive for the device, or because the object file contains an OpenACC compute construct or device routine that calls some other procedure for which no routine information was available in the initial compile. The recompile then generates an optimized object file, which is then used in the final link.

4 Examples

In this section, we use C code snippets to show how OpenACC routine propagation benefits programmers.

4.1 Propagating acc routine seq as Default

This example shows implicit device routine generation. The original code is shown in Fig. 2. The parallel region in function *test1* in file *main1.c* calls function *func1a* in file *func1.c*. Further, *func1a* calls *func1b* in that same source file. In this case the programmer omits the explicit acc routine directive from the *func1a* prototype in *main1.c* as well as from the definitions of *func1a* and *func1b* in *func1.c*. IPA recognizes the call to *func1a* in the compute construct in *test1* and marks it by default as a device routine. It then marks *func1b* as a device routine because it is called in *func1a*. Since *func1b* has no further calls, IPA will by default mark it as acc routine seq. Since *func1a* only calls one seq routine, it is marked the same way. Here, both source files are recompiled with the implicit routine directive information in both files.

```
extern float func1a( float );
    ...
void test1( float* x, int n){
    #pragma acc parallel loop copy(x[0:n])
    for( int i = 0; i < n; ++i )
        x[i] = func1a(x[i]);
}
```

(a) main1.c

```
float func1b( float* x ){
    return x%2;
}
    ...
float func1a( float* x ){
    return func1b(x) + 1;
}
```

(b) func1.c

Fig. 2. Implicit **acc routine** generation.

4.2 Propagating routine Type Across Files

Here we present two examples of IPA propagation of **acc routine** level of parallelism. The first example propagates the level of parallelism from the procedure definition to the call sites; the sample code is shown in Fig. 3. The programmer has inserted an **acc routine** directive with the **gang** clause for the function definition of *func2a* in *func21.c*. IPA propagates this annotation to the function prototype in *main2.c*. Similarly, the programmer has inserted an **acc routine** directive with the **worker** clause for the function definition of *func2b* in *func22.c*. IPA propagates this to its prototype in *func21.c*. In this case, IPA only needs to recompile the two files *main2.c* and *func21.c*, because no new information was propagated to *func22.c*.

The second example propagates the level of parallelism from a prototype declaration to the function definition; the sample code is shown in Fig. 4. Here the prototype of *func3a* in *main3.c* is annotated with **acc routine vector**. IPA propagates this annotation to the definition of *func3a* in *func3.c*. Since *func3b* has no annotation, IPA adds the default **acc routine seq** directive. Only *func3.c* is recompiled, since *main3.c* has no new information.

4.3 Detecting routine Level of Parallelism Mismatch Across Files

This example shows error detection of mismatched level of parallelism between a prototype at the call site and the definition in another file, or between two prototypes in different files; the sample code is in Fig. 5. Here the programmer

```
extern float func2a( float );
...
void test2( float* x, int n){
    #pragma acc parallel loop copy(x[0:n])
    for( int i = 0; i < n; ++i )
        x[i] = func2a(x[i]);
}
```

(a) main2.c

```
extern float func2b( float );
...
#pragma acc routine gang
float func2a( float* x ){
    return func2b(x) + 1;
}
```

(b) func21.c

```
#pragma acc routine worker
float func2b( float* x ){
    return x%2;
}
```

(c) func22.c

Fig. 3. Propagating level of parallelism from function definition to call sites.

has marked the declaration of *func4a* in *main4.c* as acc routine gang, but marked its definition in *func4.c* as acc routine vector. This could have led to incorrect execution and wrong output on execution. IPA detects this mismatch and generates an error identifying the inconsistency.

4.4 Detecting Unannotated Global Variable Usage

One additional feature of the implementation is described here in Fig. 6. In this case the function *func5a* is called from a parallel region in function *test5*. The programmer has omitted the acc routine annotation for function *func5a*, but IPA detects this and marks it by default as acc routine seq. But function *func5a* accesses the global variable *glob_y*. Since this global variable does not appear in a acc declare directive, it cannot be accessed from the device. IPA detects this and generates an appropriate error message. Without this feature, the error would have been produced in later stage where this file was being recompiled.

```
#pragma acc routine vector
float func3a( float );
  ...
void test3( float* x, int n){
   #pragma acc parallel loop copy(x[0:n])
   for( int i = 0; i < n; ++i )
      x[i] = func3a(x[i]);
}
```

(a) main3.c

```
float func3b( float* x ){
   return x%2;
}
  ...
float func3a( float* x ){
   return func3b(x) + 1;
}
```

(b) func3.c

Fig. 4. Propagating routine type from a declaration to the definition.

```
#pragma acc routine gang
extern float func4a( float );
  ...
void test4( float* x, int n){
   #pragma acc parallel loop copy(x[0:n])
   for( int i = 0; i < n; ++i )
      x[i] = func4a(x[i]);
}
```

(a) main4.c

```
#pragma acc routine vector
float func4a( float* x ){
   return x++;
}
```

(b) func4.c

Fig. 5. routine type mismatch between the definition and the declarations.

5   Summary

OpenACC requires that routines to be called on an accelerator device be annotated, so the compiler will know to generate device code for calls to them. The

```
int glob_y = 100;
...
float func5a( float* x ){
  return x*glob_y + x;
}
...
void test5( float* x, int n){
  #pragma acc parallel loop copy(x[0:n])
  for( int i = 0; i < n; ++i )
    x[i] = func5a(x[i]);
}
```

(a) main5.c

Fig. 6. Global variable inside accelerator code without declare directive.

directive annotation must also declare the level of parallelism used in that procedure, so the correct code can be made at the call site. The current OpenMP *target* directive set has an equivalent requirement. This is a cause of much frustration when porting programs, particularly for C++ programs where many calls are made to templated functions that appear in system header files that users can't modify. The specific problem for C++ programs is handled by the PGI compiler in the C++ front end, by transitively marking any unannotated procedure that can be called from an OpenACC compute construct with acc routine seq. The same mechanism could be applied to C or Fortran programs as well. However, while extremely useful, it does not address the problem of inserting these directives when the caller and callee appear in separate files.

This paper describes a semiautomatic approach to detecting and generating implicit device routine annotations across files, using interprocedural analysis. For simple procedures, IPA will mark these for single thread execution with the seq level of parallelism. For procedures that contain parallel loops, the user has to mark only the procedure definition with the appropriate level of parallelism, and IPA will propagate that to all call sites. IPA can also detect common errors, such as an invalid call site, mismatched directives for the same routine, or global variable use in an implicit device routine. While our implementation is designed for OpenACC, it could be applied equally for an OpenMP compiler that implements target offload to an accelerator device.

Our implementation is a straightforward addition to the flexible interprocedural analysis and optimization feature in the PGI compilers. Similar enhancements could be added to any compiler that implements whole program or interprocedural analysis. The major change to the PGI IPA framework is that with this feature enabled, interprocedural analysis and optimization at link time becomes required, since without the link-time propagation of the routine information, the device code will not link successfully.

There are limitations to the general procedure and limitations in our specific implementation. The implementation is based on traversal of the call graph. Indirect calls through procedure pointers generally will generate an imprecise call graph, and would require that either all possible target procedures be made available on the device, or that the user explicitly limit the set of target procedures. Our IPA implementation does not propagate information for indirect calls at this time.

Even though a programmer may not include the `routine` directive for a procedure, he or she may add `loop` directive for loops inside the routine. The `loop` directive annotations could be used to guide the level of parallelism to use for implicit device routines. Even without explicit `loop` directives, the compiler may be able to determine that a loop in a procedure could be safely executed in parallel. If such a procedure were called at sites where such parallelism could be exploited, an implementation could implicitly add a level of parallelism other than `seq`. Neither of these features is included in our implementation.

We are also exploring other situations where IPA can be used to shift work from the programmer to the compiler. One instance, specific to the PGI compiler for NVIDIA GPUs, has to do with using CUDA Managed Memory for allocatable data. The PGI compiler supports a `-ta=tesla:managed` option, which compiles the OpenACC compute constructs for execution on NVIDIA Tesla GPUs, and also replaces all dynamic memory allocation to use CUDA managed memory. Managed memory will be automatically migrated or paged between host and device memories, and thus reduces the need for OpenACC data directives and simplifies the job for the programmer. However, managed memory allocation and deallocation is relatively expensive. Currently, the `managed` suboption replaces all dynamic memory allocation. We are exploring whether we could use IPA to only replace the dynamic allocation for data that gets used in OpenACC compute constructs, using the cheaper system memory allocation for data that is only used on the host CPU.

Our IPA currently allows the compiler to automatically choose which procedures to inline, even across files. Inlining is especially beneficial for NVIDIA GPUs; the overhead of maintaining the call stack and the information lost at procedure boundaries is relatively more costly for a GPU. We are exploring optimizing the inlining decisions to prioritize inlining of procedures called in a device compute construct.

We are also exploring whether we can use IPA to find more errors at compile time. For instance, if a compute construct includes a `present` clause for some data structure, IPA might be used to determine whether there are calls to the procedure contains the compute construct where the data structure is not present, and to issue a compile-time warning or error, avoiding the need to trace this error at runtime.

Finally, we are working with the OpenACC committee to explore whether it is useful to compile multiple versions of a procedure, each with a different level of parallelism. For instance, a SAXPY procedure might be called in several different contexts. If called within a `vector` loop, the procedure must be compiled to run on a single thread in `routine seq` mode. However, if called in a `gang` loop, it could be compiled to run in parallel in `routine worker` or `routine vector` mode. We have seen at least one production application where such a feature would be useful. If that feature is added to OpenACC, then the `routine` propagation procedure would be modified to detect this situation and propagate the information appropriately.

References

1. Callahan, D., Cooper, K., Kennedy, K., Torczon, L.M.: Interprocedural constant propagation. In: Proceedings of SIGPLAN 1986 Symposium on Compiler Construction, Palo Alto, CA, pp. 152–161, June 1986
2. Chandrasekaran, S., Juckeland, G. (eds.): OpenACC for Programmers. Addison-Wesley, Boston (2018)
3. Cooper, K.: Analyzing aliases of reference formal parameters. In: Conference on Record 12th Annual ACM Symposium Principles of Programming Languages, pp. 281–290, January 1985
4. Cooper, K., Kennedy, K.: Efficient computation of flow insensitive interprocedural summary information. In: Proceedings of SIGPLAN 1984 Symposium on Compiler Construction, Montreal, Canada, pp. 247–258, June 1984
5. Cooper, K., Kennedy, K.: Fast interprocedural alias analysis. In: Proceedings of ACM SIGPLAN 1989 Conference on Principles of Programming Languages, pp. 29–41, February 1986
6. Cooper, K., Kennedy, K.: Efficient computation of flow-insensitive interprocedural summary information (a correction). Technical report TR87-60, Rice University (1987)
7. Cooper, K.D., Kennedy, K.: Interprocedural side-effect analysis in linear time. In: Proceedings of ACM SIGPLAN 1988 Conference on Programming Language Design and Implementation, Atlanta, GA, pp. 57–66, June 1988
8. CUDA toolkit documentation. http://docs.nvidia.com/cuda/
9. Farber, R. (ed.): Parallel Programming with OpenACC. Morgan Kaufmann, Boston (2017)
10. Hall, M., Kennedy, K.: Efficient call graph analysis. Lett. Program. Lang. Syst. 1(3), 227–242 (1992)
11. Nickolls, J., Buck, I., Garland, M., Skadron, K.: Scalable parallel programming with CUDA. ACM Queue 6(2), 40–53 (2008)
12. The OpenACC application programming interface, version 2.6, November 2017. https://www.openacc.org/
13. OpenCL. https://www.khronos.org/opencl/
14. The OpenMP application programming interface, version 4.5, November 2015. https://www.openmp.org/
15. Ruetsch, G., Fatica, M.: CUDA Fortran for Scientists and Engineers. Morgan Kaufmann, San Francisco (2013)

OpenACC Based GPU Parallelization
of Plane Sweep Algorithm for Geometric
Intersection

Anmol Paudel[✉] and Satish Puri

Department of Mathematics, Statistics and Computer Science,
Marquette University, Milwaukee, WI 53233, USA
{anmol.paudel,satish.puri}@marquette.edu

Abstract. Line segment intersection is one of the elementary operations
in computational geometry. Complex problems in Geographic Information Systems (GIS) like finding map overlays or spatial joins using polygonal data require solving segment intersections. Plane sweep paradigm
is used for finding geometric intersection in an efficient manner. However, it is difficult to parallelize due to its in-order processing of spatial
events. We present a new fine-grained parallel algorithm for geometric
intersection and its CPU and GPU implementation using OpenMP and
OpenACC. To the best of our knowledge, this is the first work demon-
strating an effective parallelization of plane sweep on GPUs.

We chose compiler directive based approach for implementation
because of its simplicity to parallelize sequential code. Using Nvidia Tesla
P100 GPU, our implementation achieves around 40X speedup for line
segment intersection problem on 40K and 80K data sets compared to
sequential CGAL library.

Keywords: Plane sweep · Line segment intersection ·
Directive based programming · OpenMP · OpenACC

1 Introduction

Scalable spatial computation on high performance computing (HPC) environment has been a long-standing challenge in computational geometry. Spatial
analysis using two shapefiles (4 GB) takes around ten minutes to complete using
state-of-the art desktop ArcGIS software [15]. Harnessing the massive parallelism
of graphics accelerators helps to satisfy the time-critical nature of applications
involving spatial computation. Directives-based parallelization provides an easy-
to-use mechanism to develop parallel code that can potentially reduce execution
time. Many computational geometry algorithms exhibit irregular computation
and memory access patterns. As such, parallel algorithms need to be carefully
designed to effectively run on a GPU architecture.

Geometric intersection is a class of problems involving operations on shapes
represented as line segments, rectangles (MBR), and polygons. The operations

© Springer Nature Switzerland AG 2019
S. Chandrasekaran et al. (Eds.): WACCPD 2018 Workshop, LNCS 11381, pp. 114–135, 2019.
https://doi.org/10.1007/978-3-030-12274-4_6

can be cross, overlap, contains, union, etc. Domains like Geographic Information Systems (GIS), VLSI CAD/CAM, spatial databases, etc. use geometric intersection as an elementary operation in their data analysis toolbox. Public and private sector agencies rely on spatial data analysis and spatial data mining to gain insights and produce an actionable plan [14]. We are experimenting with the line segment intersection problem because it is one of the most basic problems in spatial computing and all other operations for bigger problems like polygon overlay or polygon clipping depends on results from it. The line segment intersection problem basically asks two questions - "are the line segments intersecting or not?" and if they are intersecting "what are the points of intersection?" The first one is called intersection detection problem and the second one is called intersection reporting problem. In this paper, we present an algorithmic solution for the latter.

Plane sweep is a fundamental technique to reduce $O(n^2)$ segment to segment pair-wise computation into $O(nlogn)$ work, impacting a class of geometric problems akin to the effectiveness of FFT-based algorithms. Effective parallelization of the plane-sweep algorithm will lead to a breakthrough by enabling acceleration of computational geometry algorithms that rely on plane-sweep for efficient implementation. Examples include trapezoidal decomposition, construction of the Voronoi diagram, Delaunay triangulation, etc.

To the best of our knowledge, this is the first work on parallelizing plane sweep algorithm for geometric intersection problem on a GPU. The efficiency of plane sweep comes from its ability to restrict the search space to the immediate neighborhood of the sweepline. We have abstracted the neighbor finding algorithm using directive based reduction operations. In sequential implementations, neighbor finding algorithm is implemented using a self-balancing binary search tree which is not suitable for GPU architecture. Our multi-core and many-core implementation uses directives-based programming approach to leverage the device-specific hardware parallelism with the help of a compiler. As such the resulting code is easy to maintain and modify. With appropriate pragmas defined by OpenMP and OpenACC, the same source code will work for a CPU as well as a GPU.

In short, the paper presents the following research contributions

1. Fine-grained Parallel Algorithm for Plane Sweep based intersection problem.
2. Directives-based implementation with reduction-based approach to find neighbors in the sweeplines.
3. Performance results using OpenACC and OpenMP and comparison with sequential CGAL library. We report upto 27x speedup with OpenMP and 49x speedup with OpenACC for 80K line segments.

The rest of the paper is structured as follows. Section 2 presents a general technical background and related works to this paper. Section 3 describes our parallel algorithm. Section 4 provides details on OpenMP and OpenACC implementations. Section 5 provides experimental results. Conclusion and future work is presented in Sect. 6. Acknowledgements are in the last section.

2   Background and Related Work

There are different approaches for finding geometric intersections. In addition
to the simple brute force method, there is a filter and refine method that uses a
heuristic to avoid unnecessary intersection computations. For a larger dataset,
filter and refine strategy is preferred over brute force. Plane sweep method works
best if the dataset can fit in memory. However, the plane sweep algorithm is not
amenable to parallelization due to the in-order sequential processing of events
stored in a binary tree and a priority queue data structure. In the existing
literature, the focus of parallel algorithms in theoretical computational geometry
has been in improving the asymptotic time bounds. However, on the practical
side, there has been only a few attempts to parallelize plane sweep on multi-cores.
Moreover, those algorithms are not suitable to fine-grained SIMD parallelism in
GPUs. This has led to the parallelization of brute force algorithms with $O(n^2)$
complexity and parallelization of techniques like grid partitioning on GPUs. The
brute force algorithm that involves processing all segments against each other
is obviously embarrassingly parallel and has been implemented on GPU, but its
quadratic time complexity cannot compete even with the sequential plane sweep
for large data sets. The uniform grid technique does not perform well for skewed
data sets where segments span an arbitrary number of grid cells. Limitations in
the existing work is our motivation behind this work.

In the remaining subsections, we have provided background information
about segment intersection problem, different strategies used to solve the problem, existing work on the parallelization in this area and directive based programming.

2.1   Segment Intersection Problem

Finding line intersection in computers is not as simple as solving two mathematical equations. First of all, it has to do with how the lines are stored in the
computer – not in the $y = mx + c$ format, but rather as two endpoints like (x1,
y1, x2, y2). One reason for not storing lines in a equation format is because
most of the lines in computer applications are finite in nature, and need to have
a clear start and end points. Complex geometries like triangle, quadrilateral or
any n-vertices polygon are further stored as a bunch of points. For example a
quadrilateral would be stored like (x1, y1, x2, y2, x3, y3, x4, y4) and each sequential pair of points would form the vertices of that polygon. So, whenever we do
geometric operations using computers, we need to be aware of the datatypes
used to store the geometries, and use algorithms that can leverage them.

For non-finite lines, any two lines that are not parallel or collinear in 2D space
would eventually intersect. This is however not the case here since all the lines
we have are finite. So given two line segments we would first need to do a series
of calculation to ascertain whether they intersect or not. Since they are finite
lines, we can solve their mathematical equations to find the point of intersection
only if they intersect.

In this way we can solve the segment intersection for two lines but what if we are given a collection of line segments and are asked to find out which of these segments intersect among themselves and what are the intersection vertices. Since most complex geometries are stored as a collection of vertices which results in a collection of line segments, segment intersection detection and reporting the list of vertices of intersection are some of the most commonly solved problems in many geometric operations. Geometric operations like finding the map overlays and geometric unions all rely at their core on the results from the segment intersection problem. Faster and more efficient approaches in segment intersection will enable us to solve a wide variety of geometric operations faster and in a more efficient manner.

2.2   Naive Brute Force Approach

Like with any computational problem, the easiest approach is foremost the brute force approach. Algorithm 1 describes the brute force approach to find segment intersection among multiple lines.

Algorithm 1. Naive Brute Force

1: Load all lines to L
2: **for** each line l_1 in L **do**
3:     **for** each line l_2 in L **do**
4:         Test for intersection between l_1 and l_2
5:         **if** intersections exists **then**
6:             calculate intersection point
7:             store it in results
8:         **end if**
9:     **end for**
10: **end for**

The brute force approach works very well compared to other algorithms for the worst case scenario where all segments intersect among themselves. For N line segments, its time complexity is $O(N^2)$. This is the reason we have parallelized this algorithm here. However, if the intersections are sparse, then there are heuristics and sophisticated algorithms available. The first method is to use filter and refine heuristic which we have employed for joining two polygon layers where the line segments are taken from polygons in a layer. The second method is to apply Plane Sweep algorithm.

Filter and Refine Approach: Let us consider a geospatial operation where we have to overlay a dataset consisting of N county boundaries (polygons) on top of another dataset consisting of M lakes from USA in a Geographic Information System (GIS) to produce a third dataset consisting of all the polygons from both datasets. This operation requires $O(NM)$ pairs of polygon intersections in the worst case. However, not all county boundaries overlap with all lake boundaries.

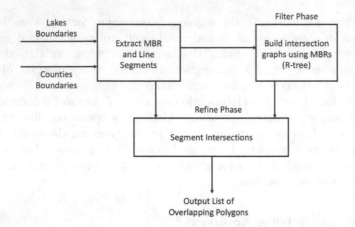

Fig. 1. Polygon intersection using filter and refine approach

This observation lends itself to filter and refine strategy where using spatial data structure like Rectangle tree (R-tree) built using bounding box approximation (MBR) of the actual boundaries, we prune the number of cross layer polygon intersections [1]. We have employed this approach while handling real spatial data. Figure 1 shows the workflow for joining two real-world datasets. The output consists of counties with lakes. The compute-intensive part here is the refine phase. Our directive based parallelization is used in the refine phase only.

2.3   Plane Sweep Algorithm

Plane sweep is an efficient algorithmic approach used in finding geometric intersections. Its time complexity is $O((N + K) \log N)$ where N is the number of line segments and K is the number of intersections found. In the worst case, K is $O(N^2)$, which makes it an $O(N^2 \log N)$ algorithm. Parallelization of plane sweep algorithm will impact many computational geometry algorithms that rely on plane-sweep for efficient implementation e.g. spatial join, polygon overlay, voronoi diagram, etc. The Bentley-Ottmann algorithm is a plane sweep algorithm, that given a collection of lines, can find out whether there are intersecting lines or not [5]. Computational geometry libraries typically use plane sweep algorithm in their implementations.

Algorithm 2 describes plane sweep using a vertical sweepline. The procedures for *HandleStartEvent*, *HandleEndEvent* and *HandleIntersectionEvent* used in Algorithm 2 are given in Algorithms 4, 5, 6 respectively. For simplicity in presentation, following assumptions are made in Algorithm 2:

1. No segment is parallel to the vertical sweeplines.
2. No intersection occurs at endpoints.
3. No more than two segments intersect in the same point.
4. No overlapping segments.

Algorithm 2. Plane Sweep

1: Load all lines to L
2: Initialize a priority queue (PQ) for sweeplines which retrieves items based on the y-position of the item
3: Insert all start and end points from L to PQ
4: Initialize a sweepline
5: While PQ is not empty:
    If the nextItem is startevent:
        The segment is added to the sweepline
        HandleStartEvent(AddedSegment)
    If the nextItem is endevent:
        The segment is removed from the sweepline
        HandleEndEvent(RemovedSegment)
    If the nextItem is intersection-event:
    [Note that there will be two contributing lines at intersection point.
    Let these two lines be l_1 and l_2.]
        HandleIntersectionEvent(l_1,l_2)
        Record the intersecting pairs

The segments that do not adhere to our assumptions in our dataset are called degenerate cases.

2.4   Existing Work on Parallelizing Segment Intersection Algorithms

Methods for finding intersections can be categorized into two classes: (i) algorithms which rely on a partitioning of the underlying space, and (ii) algorithms exploiting a spatial order defined on the segments. Plane sweep algorithm and theoretical algorithms developed around 80's and 90's fall under the second category [3,7,8]. These theoretical PRAM algorithms attain near-optimal polylogarithmic time complexity [3,7,17]. These algorithms focus on improving the asymptotic time bounds and are not practical for implementation purposes. These parallel algorithms are harder to implement because of their usage of complex tree-based data structures like parallel segment tree and hierarchical plane-sweep tree (array of trees) [4]. Moreover, tree-based algorithms may not be suitable for memory coalescing and vectorization on a GPU.

Multi-core and many-core implementation work in literature fall under the first category where the input space is partitioned for spatial data locality. The basic idea is to process different cells in parallel among threads. Based on the data distribution, existing parallel implementations of geometric intersection algorithm use uniform or adaptive grid to do domain decomposition of the input space and data [2,4,6]. Ideal grid dimension for optimal run-time is hard to determine as it depends not only on spatial data distribution, but also on hardware characteristics of the target device. Moreover, the approach of dividing the underlying space has the unfortunate consequence of effectively increasing the size of the input dataset. For instance, if an input line segment spans multiple grid cells, then the segment is simply replicated in each cell. Hence, the problem size increases considerably for finer grid resolutions. In addition to redundant computations for replicated data, in GPU with limited global memory, memory allocation for intermediate data structure to store replicated data is not space-efficient. Plane sweep does not suffer from this problem because it is an event-based algorithm.

The brute force algorithm that involves processing all line segments against each other is obviously embarrassingly parallel and has been implemented on GPU [11], but its quadratic time complexity cannot compete even with the sequential plane sweep for large data sets. Our current work is motivated by the limitations of the existing approaches which cannot guarantee efficient treatment of all possible input configurations.

Parallel algorithm developed by McKenney et al. and their OpenMP implementation is targeted towards multi-core CPUs and it is not fine-grained to exploit the SIMT parallelism in GPUs [9,10,12]. Contrary to the above-mentioned parallel algorithm, our algorithm is targeted to GPU and achieves higher speedup. In the context of massively parallel GPU platform, we have sacrificed algorithmic optimality by not using logarithmic data structures like priority queue, self-balancing binary tree and segment tree. Our approach is geared towards exploiting the concurrency available in the sequential plane sweep algorithm by adding a preprocessing step that removes the dependency among successive events.

2.5   OpenMP and OpenACC

When using compiler directives, we need to take care of data dependencies and race conditions among threads. OpenMP provides critical sections to avoid race conditions. Programmers need to remove any inter-thread dependencies from the program.

Parallelizing code for GPUs has significant differences because GPUs are separate physical devices with their numerous cores and their own separate physical memory. So, we need to first copy the spatial data from CPU to GPU to do any data processing on a GPU. Here, the CPU is regarded as the host and the GPU is regarded as the device. After processing on GPU is finished, we need to again copy back all the results from the GPU to the CPU. In GPU processing, this transfer of memory has overheads and these overheads can be large if we do multiple transfers or if the amount of memory moved is large. Also, each single GPU has its own physical memory limitations and if we have a very large dataset, then we might have to copy it to multiple GPUs or do data processing in chunks. Furthermore, the functions written for the host may not work in the GPUs and will require writing new routines. Any library modules loaded on the host device is also not available on a GPU device.

The way we achieve parallelization with OpenACC is by doing loop parallelization. In this approach each iteration of the loop can run in parallel. This can only be done if the loops have no inter-loop dependencies. Another approach we use is called vectorization. In the implementation process, we have to remove any inter-loop dependencies so that the loops can run in parallel without any side-effects. Side-effects are encountered if the threads try to write-write or write-read at the same memory location resulting in race conditions.

3   Parallel Plane Sweep Algorithm

We have taken the vertical sweep version of the Bentley-Ottmann algorithm and modified it. Instead of handling event points strictly in the increasing y-order as they are encountered in bottom-up vertical sweep, we process all the startpoints first, then all the endpoints and at last we keep on processing until there aren't any unprocessed intersection points left. During processing of each intersection event, multiple new intersection events can be found. So, the last phase of processing intersection events is iterative. Hence, the sequence of event processing is different than sequential algorithm.

Algorithm 3 describes our modified version of plane sweep using a vertical sweepline. Figure 2 shows the startevent processing for a vertical bottom up sweep. Algorithm 3 also has the same simplifying assumptions like Algorithm 2. Step 2, step 3 and the for-loop in step 4 of Algorithm 3 can be parallelized using directives.

Algorithm 3. Modified Plane Sweep Algorithm

1: Load all lines to L
2: For each line l_1 in L:
      Create a start-sweepline (SSL) at the lower point of l_1
      For each line l_2 in L:
         If l_2 crosses SSL:
            update left and right neighbors
         HandleStartEvent(l_1)
3: For each line l_1 in L:
      Create an end-sweepline (ESL) at the upper point of l_1
      For each line l_2 in L:
         If l_2 crosses ESL:
            update left and right neighbors
         HandleEndEvent(l_1)
4: While intersection events is not empty, for each intersection event:
      Create an intersection-sweepline (ISL) at the intersection point
      For each line l in L:
         If l crosses ISL:
            update left and right neighbors
         // let l_1 and l_2 are the lines at intersection event
         HandleIntersectionEvent(l_1, l_2)
5: During intersection events, we record the intersecting pairs

---

Algorithm 3 describes a fine-grained approach where each event point can be independently processed. Existing work for plane sweep focuses on coarse-grained parallelization on multi-core CPUs only. Sequential Bentley-Ottmann algorithm

---

Algorithm 4. StartEvent Processing

1: **procedure** HANDLESTARTEVENT(l_1)
    Intersection is checked between
        l_1 and its left neighbor
        l_1 and its right neighbor
    If any intersection is found
        update intersection events
2: **end procedure**

Algorithm 5. EndEvent Processing

1: **procedure** HANDLEENDEVENT(l_1)
    Intersection is checked between
        the left and right neighbors of l_1
    If intersection is found
        update intersection events
2: **end procedure**

Algorithm 6. IntersectionEvent Processing

1: **procedure** HANDLEINTERSECTIONEVENT(l_1,l_2)
    Intersection is checked between
        the left neighbor of the intersection point and l_1
        the right neighbor of the intersection point and l_1
        the left neighbor of the intersection point and l_2
        the right neighbor of the intersection point and l_2
    if any intersection is found
        update intersection events
2: **end procedure**

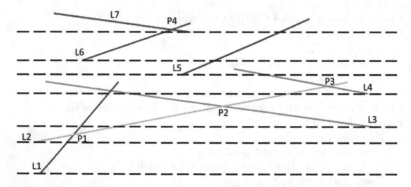

Fig. 2. Vertical plane sweep. Vertical plane sweep showing sweeplines (dotted lines) corresponding to starting event points only. P1 to P4 are the intersection vertices found by processing start event points only. L1, L2 and L3 are the active line segments on the third sweepline from the bottom. Event processing of starting point of L3 requires finding its immediate neighbor (L2) and checking doesIntersect (L2, L3) which results in finding P2 as an intersection vertex.

processes the event points as they are encountered while doing a vertical/horizontal sweep. Our parallel plane sweep relaxes the strict increasing order of event processing. Start and End point events can be processed in any order. As shown in step 4 of Algorithm 3, intersection event point processing happens after start and end point events are processed. An implementation of this algorithm either needs more memory to store line segments intersecting the sweepline or needs to compute them dynamically thereby performing more work. However, this is a necessary overhead required to eliminate the sequential dependency inherent in the original Bentley-Ottmann algorithm or its implementation. As we point out in the results section, our OpenMP and OpenACC implementations perform better than the existing work.

Degree of Concurrency: The amount of concurrency available to the algorithm is limited by Step 4 due to the fact that intersection events produce more intersection events dynamically. Hence, it results in a dependency graph where computation on each level generates a new level. The critical path length of the graph denoted by l is $0 < l < \binom{n}{2}$ where n is the input size. In general, l is less than the number of intersection points k. However, if l is comparable to k, then the Step 4 may not benefit from parallelization.

3.1   Algorithm Correctness

The novelty in this parallel algorithm is our observation that any order of concurrent events processing will produce the same results as done sequentially, provided that we schedule intersection event handling in the last phase. In a parallel implementation, this can be achieved at the expense of extra memory requirement to store the line segments per sweepline or extra computations to dynamically find out those line segments. This observation lends itself to directive based parallel programming because now we can add parallel for loop pragma in Steps 2, 3 and 4 so that we can leverage multi-core CPUs and many-core GPUs. The proof that any sweepline event needs to only consider its immediate neighbors for intersection detection is guaranteed to hold as shown by the original algorithm.

Bentley-Ottmann algorithm executes sequentially, processing each sweepline in an increasing priority order with an invariant that all the intersection points below the current sweepline has been found. However, since we process each sweepline in parallel, this will no longer be the case. The invariant in our parallel algorithm is that all line segments crossing a sweepline needs to be known a priori before doing neighborhood computation. As we can see, this is an embarrassingly parallel step.

Finally, we can show that Algorithm 3 terminates after finding all intersections. Whenever start-events are encountered they can add atmost two intersection events. End-events can add atmost one intersection event and intersection events can add atmost 4 intersection events. Because of the order in which the algorithm processes the sweeplines, all the intersection points below the current sweepline will have been found and processed. The number of iterations for Step 2 and Step 3 can be statically determined and it is linear in the number of inputs.

However, the number of iterations in Step 4 is dynamic and can be quadratic. Intersection events produce new intersection events. However, even in the worst case with $\binom{n}{2}$ intersection points generated in Step 4, the algorithm is bound to terminate.

3.2   Algorithmic Analysis

Time Complexity. For each of the N lines there will be two sweeplines, and each sweepline will have to iterate over all N lines to check if they intersect or not. So this results in $2N^2$ comparison steps, and then each intersection event will also produce a sweepline and if there are K intersection points this results in K*N steps so the total is $2N^2 + K * N$ steps. Assuming that $K \ll N$, the time-complexity of this algorithm is $O(N^2)$.

Space Complexity. Since there will be $2N$ sweeplines for N lines and for each K intersection events there will be K sweeplines. The extra memory requirement will be $O(N + K)$ and assuming $K \ll N$, the space-complexity of the algorithm is $O(N)$.

4   Directive-Based Implementation Details

Although steps 2, 3 and 4 of Algorithm 3 could run concurrently, we implemented it in such a way that each of the sweeplines within each step is processed in parallel. Also, in step 4 the intersection events are handled in batch for the ease of implementation. Furthermore, we had to make changes to the sequential code so that it could be parallelized with directives. In the sequential algorithm, the segments overlapping with a sweepline are usually stored in a data structure like BST. However, when each of the sweeplines are needed to be processed in parallel, using a data structure like the BST is not feasible so we need to apply different techniques to achieve this. In OpenMP, we can find neighbors by sorting lines in each sweepline and processing them on individual threads. Implementing the same sorting based approach is again not feasible in OpenACC because we cannot use the sorting libraries that are supported in OpenMP. So, we used a reduction-based approach supported by the reduction operators provided by OpenACC to achieve this without having to sort the lines in each sweepline.

Listing 1.1. Data structure for point

```
struct Point {
        var x,y;
        Point(var x, var y);
}
```

Listing 1.2. Data structure for line

```
struct Line {
        Point p1, p2;
        var m, c;

        Line(Point p1, Point p2) {
                m = ((p2.y - p1.y) / (p2.x - p1.x));
                c = (p1.y) - m*(p1.x);
        }
};
```

Listing 1.3. Routine for intersection point

```
#pragma acc routine
Point intersectionPoint(Line l1, Line l2) {
        var x = (l2.c - l1.c)/(l1.m - l2.m);
        var y = l1.m*x + l1.c;
        return Point(x,y);
}
```

Listing 1 shows the spatial data structures used in our implementations. The keyword *var* in the listing is meant to be a placeholder for any numeric datatype.

Finding neighboring line segments corresponding to each event efficiently is a key step in parallelizing plane sweep algorithm. In general, each sweepline has a small subset of the input line segments crossing it in an arbitrary order. The size of this subset varies across sweeplines. Finding neighbors per event would amount to sorting these subsets that are already present in global memory individually, which is not as efficient as global sorting of the overall input. Hence, we have devised an algorithm to solve this problem using directive based reduction operation. A reduction is necessary to avoid race conditions.

Algorithm 7 explains how neighbors are found using OpenACC. Each horizontal sweepline has a x-location around which the neighbors are to be found. If it is a sweepline corresponding to a startpoint or endpoint then the x-coordinate of that point will be the x-location. For a sweepline corresponding to an intersection point, the x-coordinate of the intersection point will be the x-location. To find the horizontal neighbors for the x-location, we need the x-coordinate of the intersection point between each of the input lines and the horizontal sweepline. Then a *maxloc* reduction is performed on all such intersection points that are to the left of the x-location and a *minloc* reduction is performed on all such intersection points that are to the right of the x-location to find the indices of previous and next neighbors respectively. A *maxloc* reduction finds the index of the maximum value and a *minloc* reduction finds the index of the minimum value. OpenACC doesn't directly support the *maxloc* and *minloc* operators so a workaround was implemented. The workaround includes casting the data and index combined to a larger numeric data structure for which max and min reductions are available and extracting the index from reduction results.

Figure 3 shows an example for finding two neighbors for an event with x-location as 25. The numbers shown in boxes are the x-coordinates of the intersection points of individual line segments with a sweepline (SL). We first find the index of the neighbors and then use the index to find the actual neighbors.

Algorithm 7. Reduction-based Neighbor Finding

1: Let SL be the sweepline
2: Let x be the x-coordinate in SL around which neighbors are needed
3: L ← all lines
4: prev ← MIN , nxt ← MAX
5: **for** each line l in L **do-parallel reduction(maxloc:prev, minloc:nxt)**
6:     **if** intersects(l,SL) **then**
7:         h ← intersectionPt(l,SL)
8:         **if** h < x **then**
9:             prev = h
10:        **end if**
11:        **if** h > x **then**
12:            nxt = h
13:        **end if**
14:    **end if**
15: **end for**

Polygon Intersection Using Filter and Refine Approach: As discussed earlier, joining two polygon layers to produce third layer as output requires a filter phase where we find pairs of overlapping polygons from the two input layers. The filter phase is data-intensive in nature and it is carried out in CPU. The next refine phase carries out pair-wise polygon intersection. Typically, on a dataset of a few gigabytes, there can be thousands to millions of such polygon pairs where a polygon intersection routine can be invoked to process an individual pair. First, we create a spatial index (R-tree) using minimum bounding rectangles (MBRs) of polygons of one layer and then perform R-tree queries using MBRs of another layer to find overlapping cross-layer polygons. We first tried a fine-grained parallelization scheme with a pair of overlapping polygons as an OpenMP task. But this approach did not perform well due to significantly large number of tasks. A coarse-grained approach where a task is a pair consisting of a polygon from one layer and a list of overlapping polygons from another layer performed better. These tasks are independent and processed in parallel by OpenMP due to typically large number of tasks to keep the multi-cores busy.

We used sequential Geometry Opensource (GEOS) library for R-tree construction, MBR querying and polygon intersection functions. Here, intersection function uses sequential plane-sweep algorithm to find segment intersections. We tried naive all-to-all segment intersection algorithm with OpenMP but it is slower than plane sweep based implementation. Our OpenMP implementation is based on thread-safe C API provided by GEOS. We have used the Prepared-

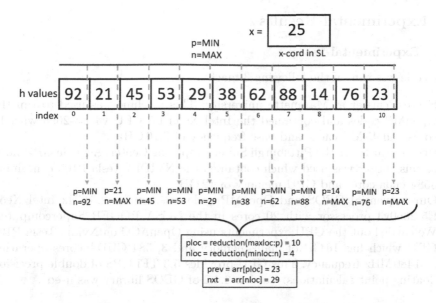

Fig. 3. Reduction-based neighbor finding. Here the dotted lines are the parallel threads and we find the left and right neighbor to the given x-cord (25) on the sweepline and their corresponding indices. p and n are thread local variables that are initialized as MIN and MAX respectively. As the threads execute concurrently their value gets independently updated based on Algorithm 7.

Geometry class which is an optimized version of Geometry class designed for filter-and-refine use cases.

Hybrid CPU-GPU Parallelization: Only the refine phase is suitable for GPU parallelization because it involves millions of segment intersections tests for large datasets. Creating intersection graph to identify overlapping polygons is carried out on CPU. The intersection graph is copied to the GPU using OpenACC data directives. The segment intersection algorithm used in OpenACC is the brute force algorithm. We cannot simply add pragmas to GEOS code. This is due to the fact that OpenACC is not designed to run sophisticated plane sweep algorithm efficiently. For efficiency, the code needs to be vectorized by the PGI compiler and allow Single Instruction Multiple Thread (SIMT) parallelization. Directive-based loop parallelism using *OpenACC parallel for* construct is used. The segment intersection computation for the tasks generated by filter phase are carried out in three nested loops. Outermost loop iterates over all the tasks. Two inner for loops carry out naive all-to-all edge intersection tests for a polygon pair.

5   Experimental Results

5.1   Experimental Setup

Our code was run on the following 3 machines:

- Everest cluster at Marquette university: This machine was used to run the OpenMP codes and contained the Intel Xeon E5 CPU v4 E5-2695 with 18 cores and 45 MB cache and base frequency of 2.10 GHz.
- Bridges cluster at the Pittsburgh Supercomputing Center: A single GPU node of this cluster was used which contained the NVIDIA Tesla P100 containing 3584 cuda cores and GPU memory of 12 GB.
- Our sequential GEOS and OpenMP code was run on 2.6 GHz Intel Xeon E5-2660v3 processor with 20 cores in the NCSA ROGER Supercomputer. We carried out the GPU experiments using OpenACC on Nvidia Tesla P100 GPU which has 16 GB of main memory and 3,584 CUDA cores operating at 1480 MHz frequency. This GPU provides 5.3 TFLOPS of double precision floating point calculations. Version 3.4.2 of GEOS library was used[1].

Dataset Descriptions: We have used artificially generated and real spatial datasets for performance evaluation.

Generated Dataset: Random lines were generated for performance measurement and collecting timing information. Datasets vary in the number of lines generated. Sparsity of data was controlled during data set generation to have about only 10% of intersections. Table 1 shows the datasets we generated and used and the number of intersections in each dataset. The datasets are sparsely distributed and number of intersections are only about 10% of the number of lines in the dataset. Figure 4 depicts a randomly generated set of sparse lines.

Real-World Spatial Datasets: As real-world spatial data, we selected polygonal data from Geographic Information System (GIS) domain[2,3] [13]. The details of the datasets are provided in Table 2.

Table 1. Dataset and corresponding number of intersections

Lines	Intersections
10k	1095
20k	2068
40k	4078
80k	8062

---

[1] https://trac.osgeo.org/geos/.
[2] http://www.naturalearthdata.com.
[3] http://resources.arcgis.com.

Fig. 4. Randomly generated sparse lines

Table 2. Description of real-world datasets.

	Dataset	Polygons	Edges	Size
1	Urban areas	11K	1,153K	20 MB
2	State provinces	4K	1,332K	50 MB
3	Sports areas	1,783K	20,692K	590 MB
4	Postal code areas	170K	65,269K	1.4 GB
5	Water bodies	463K	24,201K	520 MB
6	Block boundaries	219K	60,046K	1.3 GB

5.2   Performance of Brute Force Parallel Algorithm

Using Generated Dataset: Table 3 shows execution time comparison of
CGAL, sequential brute-force (BF-Seq) and OpenACC augmented brute-force
(BF-ACC) implementations.

Key takeaway from the Table 3 is that CGAL performs significantly better
than our naive code for sparse set of lines in sequential and the increase in
sequential time is not linear with the increase in data size. OpenACC however
drastically beats the sequential performance especially for larger data sizes.

Table 3. Execution time by CGAL, naive Sequential vs OpenACC on sparse lines

Lines	CGAL	BF-Seq	BF-ACC
10k	3.96 s	8.19 s	0.6 s
20k	9.64 s	35.52 s	1.52 s
40k	17.23 s	143.94 s	5.02 s
80k	36.45 s	204.94 s	6.73 s

Using Real Polygonal Dataset: Here the line segments are taken from the polygons. The polygon intersection tests are distributed among CPU threads in static, dynamic and guided load-balancing modes supported by OpenMP. Table 4 shows the execution time for polygon intersection operation using three real-world shapefiles listed in Table 2. The performance of GEOS-OpenMP depends on number of threads, chunk size and thread scheduling. We varied these parameters to get the best performance for comparison with GEOS. For the largest data set, chunk size as 100 and dynamic loop scheduling yielded the best speedup for 20 threads. We see better performance using real datasets as well when compared to optimized opensource GIS library.

For polygonal data, OpenACC version is about two to five times faster than OpenMP version even though it is running brute force algorithm for the refine phase. The timing includes data transfer time. When compared to the sequential library, it is four to eight times faster.

Table 4. Performance comparison of polygon intersection operation using sequential and parallel methods on real-world datasets.

Dataset	Running time (s)		
	Sequential	Parallel	
	GEOS	OpenMP	OpenACC
Urban-States	5.77	2.63	1.21
USA-Blocks-Water	148.04	83.10	34.69
Sports-Postal-Areas	267.34	173.51	31.82

5.3 Performance of Parallel Plane Sweep Algorithm

Table 5 shows the scalability of parallel plane sweep algorithm using OpenMP on Intel Xeon E5. Table 6 is comparison of CGAL and parallel plane sweep (PS-ACC). Key takeaway from the Table 6 is that for the given size of datasets the parallel plane sweep in OpenACC drastically beats the sequential performance of CGAL or the other sequential method as shown in Table 3.

Table 5. Parallel plane sweep on sparse lines with OpenMP

Lines	1p	2p	4p	8p	16p	32p
10k	1.9 s	1.22 s	0.65 s	0.37 s	0.21 s	0.13 s
20k	5.76 s	3.24 s	1.78 s	1.08 s	0.66 s	0.37 s
40k	20.98 s	11.01 s	5.77 s	3.3 s	2.03 s	1.14 s
80k	82.96 s	42.3 s	21.44 s	12.18 s	6.91 s	3.78 s

Table 6. CGAL vs OpenACC parallel plane sweep on sparse lines

Lines	CGAL	PS-ACC
10k	3.96 s	0.33 s
20k	9.64 s	0.34 s
40k	17.23 s	0.41 s
80k	36.45 s	0.74 s

Table 7. Speedup with OpenACC when compared to CGAL for different datasets

	10K	20K	40K	80K
BF-ACC	6.6	6.34	3.43	5.42
PS-ACC	12	28.35	42.02	49.26

5.4   Speedup and Efficiency Comparisons

Table 7 shows the speedup gained when comparing CGAL with the OpenACC implementation of the brute force (BF-ACC) and plane sweep approaches (PS-ACC) on NVIDIA Tesla P100. Figure 5 shows the time taken for computing intersection on sparse lines in comparison to OpenACC based implementations with CGAL and sequential brute force. The results with directives are promising because even the brute force approach gives around a 5x speedup for 80K lines. Moreover, our parallel implementation of plane sweep gives a 49x speedup.

Figure 6 shows the speedup with varying number of threads and it validates the parallelization of the parallel plane sweep approach. The speedup is consistent with the increase in the number of threads. Figure 7 shows the efficiency (speedup/threads) for the previous speedup graph. As we can see in the figure,

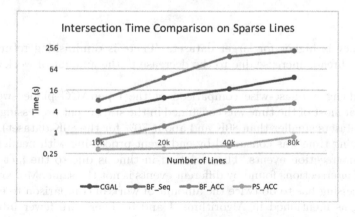

Fig. 5. Time comparison for CGAL, sequential brute-force, OpenACC augmented brute-force and plane sweep on sparse lines

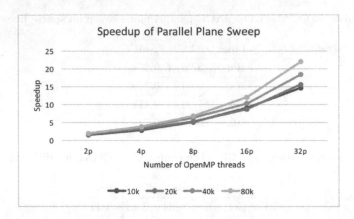

Fig. 6. Speedups for the parallel plane sweep with varying OpenMP threads on sparse lines

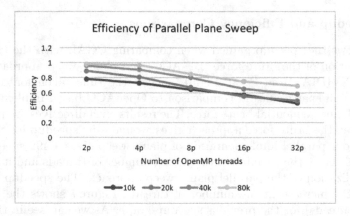

Fig. 7. Efficiency of the parallel plane sweep with varying OpenMP threads on sparse lines

the efficiency is higher for larger datasets. There is diminishing return as the number of threads increase due to the decrease in the amount of work available per thread.

Also, doing a phase-wise comparison of the OpenACC plane sweep code showed that most of the time was consumed in the start event processing (around 90% for datasets smaller than 80K and about 70% for the 80K dataset). Most of the remaining time was consumed by end event processing with negligible time spent on intersection events. The variation in time is due to the fact that the number of intersections found by different events is not the same. Moreover, start event processing has to do twice the amount of work in comparison to end event processing as mentioned in Algorithms 4 and 5. There are fewer intersection point events in comparison to the endpoint events.

6   Conclusion and Future Work

In this work, we presented a fine-grained parallel algorithm targeted to GPU architecture for a non-trivial computational geometry code. We also presented an efficient implementation using OpenACC directives that leverages GPU parallelism. This has resulted in an order of magnitude speedup compared to the sequential implementations. We have also shown our compiler directives based parallelization method using real polygonal data. We are planning to integrate the present work with our MPI-GIS software so that we can handle larger datasets and utilize multiple GPUs [16].

Compiler directives prove to be a promising avenue to explore in the future for parallelizing other spatial computations as well. Although in this paper we have not handled the degenerate cases for plane sweep algorithm, they can be dealt with the same way we would deal with degenerate cases in the sequential plane sweep approach. Degenerate cases arise due to the assumptions that we had made in the plansweep algorithm. However, it remains one of our future work to explore parallel and directive based methods to handle such cases.

Acknowledgements. This work is partly supported by the National Science Foundation CRII Grant No. 1756000. We gratefully acknowledge the support of NVIDIA Corporation with the donation of the Titan X Pascal GPU used for this research. We also acknowledge XSEDE for providing access to NVidia Tesla P100 available in PSC Bridges cluster.

Appendix A Artifact Description Appendix

A.1 Description

Check-List (Artifact Meta Information)

- **Algorithm:**
  All algorithms are mentioned and described in the paper itself and can be referred to in Algorithms 1 and 3.
- **Program:**
  The Computational Geometry Algorithms Library (CGAL) and Geometry Engine Open Source (GEOS) were external libraries that were used.
- **Compilation:**
  Compilations were done using the g++ compiler and pgc++ compilers.
  for OpenACC: pgc++ -acc -ta=tesla:cc60 -o prog prog.cpp
  for OpenMP: g++ -fopenmp -o prog prog.cpp
  for CGAL: g++ -lcgal -o prog prog.cpp
  for GEOS: g++ -lgeos -o prog prog.cpp
- **Hardware:**
  Description of the machines used to run code can be found in Sect. 5.1 for further information.
- **Publicly available:**
  CGAL, GEOS, OpenMP, OpenACC, gcc and pgcc are all publicly available.

How Software Can Be Obtained (if Available). All of the software and code we used to build up our experiments were freely and publicly available. However, our code implementation can be found in the website: https://www.mscs.mu.edu/~satish/mpiaccgis.html.

Hardware Dependencies. To be able to get the most out of OpenMP, a multicore CPU would be needed. And to be able to run OpenACC kernels a GPU would be needed.

Software Dependencies. CGAL, GEOS, OpenMP and OpenACC libraries must be installed. Compilers like gcc and pgcc are also needed.

Datasets. Real world spatial data were used and datasets containing random lines were generated. Please refer to Sect. 5.1 for more information. Generated datasets are also posted in the website: https://www.mscs.mu.edu/~satish/mpiaccgis.html, however they can be generated on your own.

A.2 Installation

1. Configure the multicore CPUs and GPU to run on your system
2. Install the necessary libraries
3. Download or generate the necessary datasets
4. Download the code
5. Check that the datasets are in the proper directory pointed by the code, if not then fix it
6. Compile the code
7. Execute the compiled executable

References

1. Agarwal, D., Puri, S., He, X., Prasad, S.K.: A system for GIS polygonal overlay computation on linux cluster - an experience and performance report. In: 26th IEEE International Parallel and Distributed Processing Symposium Workshops & PhD Forum, IPDPS 2012, Shanghai, China, 21–25 May 2012, pp. 1433–1439 (2012). https://doi.org/10.1109/IPDPSW.2012.180
2. Aghajarian, D., Prasad, S.K.: A spatial join algorithm based on a non-uniform grid technique over GPGPU. In: Proceedings of the 25th ACM SIGSPATIAL International Conference on Advances in Geographic Information Systems, p. 56. ACM (2017)
3. Atallah, M.J., Goodrich, M.T.: Efficient plane sweeping in parallel. In: Proceedings of the Second Annual Symposium on Computational Geometry, pp. 216–225. ACM (1986)
4. Audet, S., Albertsson, C., Murase, M., Asahara, A.: Robust and efficient polygon overlay on parallel stream processors. In: Proceedings of the 21st ACM SIGSPATIAL International Conference on Advances in Geographic Information Systems, pp. 304–313. ACM (2013)

5. Bentley, J.L., Ottmann, T.A.: Algorithms for reporting and counting geometric intersections. IEEE Trans. Comput. **9**, 643–647 (1979)
6. Franklin, W.R., Narayanaswami, C., Kankanhalli, M., Sun, D., Zhou, M.C., Wu, P.Y.: Uniform grids: a technique for intersection detection on serial and parallel machines. In: Proceedings of Auto Carto, vol. 9, pp. 100–109. Citeseer (1989)
7. Goodrich, M.T.: Intersecting line segments in parallel with an output-sensitive number of processors. SIAM J. Comput. **20**(4), 737–755 (1991)
8. Goodrich, M.T., Ghouse, M.R., Bright, J.: Sweep methods for parallel computational geometry. Algorithmica **15**(2), 126–153 (1996)
9. Khlopotine, A.B., Jandhyala, V., Kirkpatrick, D.: A variant of parallel plane sweep algorithm for multicore systems. IEEE Trans. Comput.-Aided Des. Integr. Circ. Syst. **32**(6), 966–970 (2013)
10. McKenney, M., Frye, R., Dellamano, M., Anderson, K., Harris, J.: Multi-core parallelism for plane sweep algorithms as a foundation for GIS operations. GeoInformatica **21**(1), 151–174 (2017)
11. McKenney, M., De Luna, G., Hill, S., Lowell, L.: Geospatial overlay computation on the GPU. In: Proceedings of the 19th ACM SIGSPATIAL International Conference on Advances in Geographic Information Systems, pp. 473–476. ACM (2011)
12. McKenney, M., McGuire, T.: A parallel plane sweep algorithm for multi-core systems. In: Proceedings of the 17th ACM SIGSPATIAL International Conference on Advances in Geographic Information Systems, pp. 392–395. ACM (2009)
13. OSM: OpenStreet Map Data (2017). http://spatialhadoop.cs.umn.edu/datasets.html
14. Prasad, S., et al.: Parallel processing over spatial-temporal datasets from geo, bio, climate and social science communities: a research roadmap. In: 6th IEEE International Congress on Big Data, Hawaii (2017)
15. Puri, S., Prasad, S.K.: A parallel algorithm for clipping polygons with improved bounds and a distributed overlay processing system using MPI. In: 2015 15th IEEE/ACM International Symposium on Cluster, Cloud and Grid Computing (CCGrid)(CCGRID), pp. 576–585, May 2015. https://doi.org/10.1109/CCGrid.2015.43
16. Puri, S., Paudel, A., Prasad, S.K.: MPI-vector-IO: parallel I/O and partitioning for geospatial vector data. In: Proceedings of the 47th International Conference on Parallel Processing, ICPP 2018, pp. 13:1–13:11. ACM, New York (2018). https://doi.org/10.1145/3225058.3225105
17. Puri, S., Prasad, S.K.: Output-sensitive parallel algorithm for polygon clipping. In: 43rd International Conference on Parallel Processing, ICPP 2014, Minneapolis, MN, USA, 9–12 September 2014, pp. 241–250 (2014). https://doi.org/10.1109/ICPP.2014.33

Author Index

Printed in the United States
By Bookmasters